take 5

150 five-ingredient recipes

**WEIGHT WATCHERS
PUBLISHING GROUP**

Creative and Editorial Director
Nancy Gagliardi

Art Director
Ed Melnitsky

Production Manager
Alan Biederman

Office Manager/Publishing Assistant
Jenny Laboy-Brace

Food Editor
Carol Prager

Recipe Developers
David Bonom
Cynthia DePersio
Paul Picciuto
Mark Scarbrough
Bruce Weinstein

Photographer
Ann Stratton

Food Stylist
Michael Pederson

Prop Stylist
Cathy Cook

Illustrator
Bob Eckstein

Designer
Mim Adkins

Editorial Consultant
Barbara Turvett

A Word About Weight Watchers

Since 1963, Weight Watchers has grown from a handful of people to millions of enrollments annually. Today, Weight Watchers is recognized as the leading name in safe and sensible weight control. Weight Watchers members form a diverse group, from youths to senior citizens, attending meetings virtually around the globe. Weight-loss and weight-management results vary by individual, but we recommend that you attend Weight Watchers meetings, follow the Weight Watchers food plan, and participate in regular physical activity. For a Weight Watchers meeting near you, call 800-651-6000. Also, check out *Weight Watchers* Magazine (for subscription information call 800-978-2400) and visit us at our Web site: WeightWatchers.com.

Icons

- hot/fiery
- no cooking
- one pot
- 20 minutes or less
- vegetarian

contents

Introduction

I admit it. My book shelves are lined with cookbooks—beautiful, comprehensive, inspired books that transport me to a few places I've visited, as well as the many more on my "Must Get To" list. If I have a hankering for Spanish tapas, I can whip up Boquerones en Vinagre (marinated anchovies). A yen for spicy Southeast Asian fare? Then I try Malaysian Fish Cakes or Spicy Thai Shrimp Satay. Craving an Indian feast? I may start with Chicken Tandoori and Coconut Rice Pilaf. And the list of exotic fare from these wonderful books goes on and on.

While I love experimenting with new flavors, I lack the one thing that's crucial for this type of creative cooking: time. It's when I'm heading home from the office that I ask myself, "What's for dinner?" Take-out is easy, fast, and oftentimes quite good. But a steady diet of cart-it-home cuisine just isn't smart when you're trying to shed pounds or maintain weight loss. The fact is, my dinnertime repertoire generally revolves around one book (yes, it's a Weight Watchers cookbook), which is supplemented and stuffed with pages that have been torn, snipped, or copied from other resources. When dinnertime is looming I start sifting through the recipes, keeping a few things in mind: first, what's currently in my cupboard or fridge; second, how many ingredients I'm missing for the recipe I want to make (read: how quickly can I get in and out of the grocery store?); and third, what will satisfy tonight's particular hankering. My cooking radar is also keyed into size: How long is the recipe? The ingredients list? The cooking time called for?

This kamikaze, take-no-prisoners approach is about getting a nutritious and delicious meal on the table as quickly as possible. Sound familiar? If yes, then we think you'll appreciate and use *Weight Watchers Take 5: 150 Great Five-Ingredient Recipes!* When we were developing this book and I reviewed the recipe list, I was skeptical. The recipes sounded so good, I honestly felt there was no way we could live up to our claim of no more than five ingredients in each. But with a well-stocked pantry and freezer, many of these dishes are absolutely doable—fast, easy, and delicious. If you're skeptical about the five-ingredient promise, I'll come clean up front: We generally aren't counting salt and pepper. Otherwise, you'll find that these recipes come through with flying colors.

Naturally, we've added what you've come to expect from our cookbooks: scads of tips and ideas that give you an edge if you're missing an ingredient or need to shave minutes from your prep or cooking time. We've included suggestions for pairing main dishes with sides, many helpful kitchen an shopping hints, and, of course, complete nutrition analysis and ***POINTS*** values.

I'm convinced that after you page through *Weight Watchers Take 5: 150 Great Five-Ingredient Recipes!* you'll make this one of those keeper cookbooks that become dog-eared and stained over time...the sign of a real—and really good—cookbook.

Best,
Nancy Gagliardi
Editorial Director

Chapter 1

salad days

tasty tossed entrées and sides

QUICK LIST

Belgian endive
radicchio
arugula
extra-virgin olive oil
balsamic vinegar

Tricolori Salad

MAKES 4 SERVINGS

This three-colored salad is a tradition in New York City's Italian-American restaurants. To keep the greens from wilting, toss them first with the olive oil to coat and protect them; then toss them with the vinegar. To shred the lettuces, trim the arugula and the bottoms off the endive and radicchio. Then, using a chef's knife, make cuts that are perpendicular to the leaves, every half inch.

1 medium Belgian endive, shredded
1 small radicchio, shredded
3 cups packed arugula, shredded
2 tablespoons extra-virgin olive oil
2 tablespoons balsamic vinegar (preferably aged)
½ teaspoon salt
½ teaspoon freshly ground pepper

Toss the endive, radicchio, and arugula with the oil in a large bowl. Add the vinegar, salt, and pepper; gently toss to coat. Serve at once.

Per serving (about 1 cup): 86 Cal, 7 g Fat, 1 g Sat Fat, 0 mg Chol, 315 mg Sod, 5 g Carb, 2 g Fib, 2 g Prot, 51 mg Calc. ***POINTS: 2.***

FIVE-STAR TIP   Use extra-virgin olive oil, as well as the best aged balsamic vinegar you can comfortably afford. Their sweetness and tang are the perfect finish for these earthy greens.

baby greens
blueberries
peaches
sunflower seeds
ginger vinaigrette

QUICK LIST

Tossed Greens with Summer Fruit

MAKES 4 SERVINGS

Here's a refreshing toss of greens, fruit, and seeds perfectly suited for warm weather. But you can also enjoy it year-round by substituting frozen blueberries and peach slices. Use packaged spring or mesclun salad mix from the produce aisle to make the prep a breeze.

4 cups rinsed baby greens
1 cup fresh blueberries
   (about ½ pint)
2 medium peaches, peeled
   and thinly sliced
2 tablespoons unsalted
   sunflower seeds
¼ cup low-fat ginger
   vinaigrette (e.g., Annie's
   Naturals Low-Fat Gingerly
   Dressing)

Combine the greens, blueberries, sliced peaches, and sunflower seeds in a large bowl. Drizzle with the dressing and toss gently to coat.

Per serving (1½ cups): 94 Cal, 3 g Fat, 0 g Sat Fat, 0 mg Chol, 151 mg Sod, 15 g Carb, 4 g Fib, 3 g Prot, 38 mg Calc. **_POINTS: 1._**

FIVE-STAR TIP   For a light entrée, top the salad with ¼ pound cooked sliced chicken (just add another **_1 POINT_** per serving). Feel free to use any variety of low-fat salad dressing for this recipe. Low-fat raspberry, honey mustard, or mango are all good choices.

QUICK LIST

Belgian endive
pimientos
artichoke hearts
toasted walnuts
lemon juice

Shredded Endive Salad

MAKES 6 SERVINGS

Pimientos and marinated artichokes provide a colorful, textural contrast to the crisp endive in this deceptively easy-to-make salad. The result: an elegant dish with great flavor. To shred the endive, trim the bottoms, then make cuts that are perpendicular to the leaves, every half inch. This dish beautifully compliments our Stuffed Chicken Breasts with Prosciutto and Fontina [see page 118].

2 large Belgian endive, shredded (about 6 ounces each)

1 (4-ounce) jar water-packed sliced pimientos, drained and coarsely chopped

1 (6-ounce) jar marinated artichoke hearts, drained and coarsely chopped

3 tablespoons chopped toasted walnuts

½ teaspoon freshly ground pepper

¼ cup fresh lemon juice

Combine the endive, pimientos, artichoke hearts, walnuts, and pepper in a large bowl. Add the lemon juice; toss gently to coat. Serve at once.

Per serving (1 cup): 60 Cal, 4 g Fat, 0 g Sat Fat, 0 mg Chol, 95 mg Sod, 7 g Carb, 3 g Fib, 2 g Prot, 33 mg Calc. **POINTS: 1.**

FIVE-STAR TIP Belgian endive, a close cousin of chicory, was once a seasonal treat—harvested in late November, from plants forced to grow in complete darkness to keep them from turning green. Thanks to modern agriculture, it can now be enjoyed year-round. Buy tightly packed heads, with pale yellow-green tips. Endive turns bitter when exposed to the light, so wrap it in paper towels and store it in a plastic bag in the refrigerator.

Shredded Endive Salad and
Stuffed Chicken Breasts with
Prosciutto and Fontina

QUICK LIST

cantaloupe
honeydew melon
watermelon
blueberries
poppy seed dressing

Melon-Berry Salad with Poppy Seed Dressing

MAKES 4 SERVINGS

Include this fresh and light salad in a festive Sunday brunch, or enjoy it on tossed salad greens as a quick meal any day of the week. Use whatever variety of melons or berries that looks best at the market. To save time, you can buy precut melon pieces from the produce aisle, or even use frozen melon balls (but you'll need to defrost them before proceeding with the recipe).

1 cup finely diced cantaloupe
1 cup finely diced honeydew melon
1 cup finely diced watermelon
1 cup fresh blueberries (about ½ pint)
¼ cup fat-free poppy seed dressing (e.g., Rosmarino's Honey-Poppy Seed Dressing)

Combine the cantaloupe, honeydew melon, watermelon, and blueberries in a large bowl. Drizzle the fruit with the poppy seed dressing; toss gently to coat. Serve at once.

Per serving (1 cup): 76 Cal, 1 g Fat, 0 g Sat Fat, 0 mg Chol, 131 mg Sod, 19 g Carb, 6 g Fib, 1 g Prot, 13 mg Calc. ***POINTS: 1.***

FIVE-STAR TIP This recipe can easily be doubled for a crowd. The melon can be cut up and refrigerated in an airtight container overnight, then tossed with the blueberries and the dressing just before serving.

cucumbers
red onion
golden raisins
dill
fat-free yogurt

QUICK LIST

Cucumber-Yogurt Salad

MAKES 4 SERVINGS

This palate-pleasing salad, with a touch of golden raisins for sweetness, gets its inspiration from raita, a classic Indian condiment. It can easily be doubled or tripled, if you want to serve it as part of a buffet. Because the cucumbers "weep," the salad is best eaten the day it's made. To prep the cucumbers, cut them lengthwise in half, then use a grapefruit spoon to scrape out the seeds.

3 medium cucumbers, peeled, seeded, and cut into ¼-inch-thick slices

1 small red onion, minced

⅓ cup golden raisins, chopped

2 tablespoons minced dill

½ teaspoon freshly ground pepper

¼ teaspoon salt

1 cup plain fat-free yogurt

Combine the cucumbers, onion, raisins, dill, pepper, and salt in a large bowl. Pour the yogurt over the top and toss gently to coat.

Per serving (1¼ cups): 89 Cal, 0 g Fat, 0 g Sat Fat, 1 mg Chol, 184 mg Sod, 20 g Carb, 2 g Fib, 4 g Prot, 107 mg Calc. **POINTS: 1.**

QUICK LIST

grapefruit juice
honey mustard
zucchini
yellow squash
walnuts

Confetti Squash Salad

MAKES 4 SERVINGS

Because the zucchini and yellow squash lose their crunch soon after this colorful salad is dressed, the dish won't keep for long. Thankfully, it's a snap to make, ready in minutes. Use a box grater or a food processor fitted with a shredding blade to prep the squash.

⅓ cup fresh grapefruit juice
1 tablespoon honey mustard
¼ teaspoon salt
¼ teaspoon freshly ground pepper
1 large zucchini, shredded
1 large yellow squash, shredded
⅓ cup chopped toasted walnuts

Whisk the grapefruit juice, honey mustard, salt, and pepper in a large bowl until well blended. Add the zucchini, yellow squash, and walnuts; toss gently to coat.

Per serving (1 cup): 105 Cal, 7 g Fat, 1 g Sat Fat, 0 mg Chol, 157 mg Sod, 9 g Carb, 3 g Fib, 3 g Prot, 34 mg Calc. *POINTS: 2.*

FIVE-STAR TIP To toast the walnuts, place them in a small skillet over medium-low heat; shake the pan and stir constantly until fragrant, 3 to 5 minutes.

QUICK LIST

red potatoes
smoked turkey breast
scallions
caraway seeds
sauerkraut

German Potato-Cabbage Salad

MAKES 4 SERVINGS

This lively main-dish salad gets its piquant taste from prepared sauerkraut. Low-sodium sauerkraut is available fresh in the produce section of most supermarkets. Do not drain it, since the juice makes the dressing.

8 small red potatoes, rinsed

1 (¼-pound) piece smoked turkey breast, cut into ½-inch pieces

2 scallions, thinly sliced

1½ teaspoons caraway seeds, crushed

12 ounces low-sodium sauerkraut with juice (about 2 cups)

1. Combine the potatoes in a saucepan with enough water to cover and bring to a boil. Simmer until the potatoes are tender enough to be pierced with a knife, about 12 minutes. Drain, cool 5 minutes, and cut into quarters.

2. Combine the potatoes, turkey, scallions, and caraway in a large bowl. Add the sauerkraut and toss gently to coat.

Per serving (1 cup): 122 Cal, 1 g Fat, 0 g Sat Fat, 12 mg Chol, 527 mg Sod, 20 g Carb, 5 g Fib, 9 g Prot, 43 mg Calc. *POINTS: 2.*

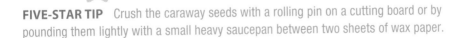

FIVE-STAR TIP Crush the caraway seeds with a rolling pin on a cutting board or by pounding them lightly with a small heavy saucepan between two sheets of wax paper.

poblano chile
romaine lettuce
jicama
cherry tomatoes
corn relish

South-of-the-Border Corn Salad

MAKES 6 SERVINGS

The poblano chile, indigenous to central Mexico for almost 4,000 years, is what gives this salad its snap. Poblanos range from green to brown—the darker the skin, the deeper and spicier the taste. They can be found in Mexican or Latin-American markets, as well as in many larger grocery stores. You'll say "Olé!" when you serve this alongside Broiled Tex-Mex Steak [see page 39].

1 large poblano chile

4 cups chopped romaine lettuce (about 8 large leaves)

2 cups peeled and shredded jicama (about ½ pound)

16 cherry tomatoes, halved

6 tablespoons low-sodium corn relish (e.g., Stonewall Kitchen's Corn Relish)

1. Preheat the broiler. Line a small baking sheet with foil; place the chile on the baking sheet. Broil 5 inches from the heat, turning with tongs, until charred, about 5 minutes. Wrap the chile in foil and let steam 15 minutes. When cool enough to handle, peel, discard the seeds, and coarsely chop.

2. Combine the roasted poblano, lettuce, jicama, tomatoes, and corn relish in a large bowl. Serve at once.

Per serving (1 cup): 63 Cal, 0 g Fat, 0 g Sat Fat, 0 mg Chol, 104 mg Sod, 14 g Carb, 3 g Fib, 1 g Prot, 21 mg Calc. **POINTS: 1.**

FIVE-STAR TIP   To shred the jicama, use a box grater. Or, if you prefer, cut the jicama into matchstick-size pieces. This salad can be stored, covered, in the refrigerator for up to two days.

South-of-the-Border
Corn Salad and
Broiled Tex-Mex Steak

QUICK LIST

tomatoes
celery
bean sprouts
fat-free mayonnaise
curry powder

Stuffed Tomato Cups

MAKES 4 SERVINGS

Here's a dish elegant enough to have been served at one of your grandmother's fanciest luncheons. But these ruby tomato cups, heaping with curried salad, are so easy to make, why wait for a special occasion? For a lavish light entrée, add ¼ pound diced cooked chicken or shrimp to the filling along with 1 additional tablespoon fat-free mayonnaise (your new tab will be *2 POINTS* for each serving).

4 large tomatoes
4 celery stalks, minced
1 cup bean sprouts
¼ cup fat-free mayonnaise
1½ teaspoons curry powder

1. With a sharp knife, slice off the top inch of each tomato. With a grapefruit spoon or a small spoon, scoop out the pulp, leaving about ¼ inch of the tomato shell. Drain the pulp in a fine-mesh sieve for 10 minutes; set the tomato cups aside.
2. Finely chop the drained tomato pulp and place in a medium bowl; stir in the celery and bean sprouts.
3. Whisk the mayonnaise and curry powder in a small bowl. Pour over the tomato mixture and toss to coat.
4. Mound the filling into the reserved tomato cups.

Per serving (1 stuffed tomato): 79 Cal, 1 g Fat, 0 g Sat Fat, 2 mg Chol, 190 mg Sod, 17 g Carb, 5 g Fib, 4 g Prot, 38 mg Calc. *POINTS: 1.*

FIVE-STAR TIP If your tomatoes are small, mound any excess salad on the plate around them. For a spicier taste, use radish sprouts instead of bean sprouts. This salad can be stored, covered, in the refrigerator up to 24 hours.

	QUICK LIST
golden beets	
turnips	
carrots	
olive oil	
balsamic vinegar	

Roasted Roots

MAKES 6 SERVINGS

With earthy root vegetables slow-roasted to perfection, this easy salad may taste like winter. But it's also perfect in the summer, along with a glass of sparkling water and fresh berries for dessert. Use a large roasting pan for the vegetables, so they won't steam from lying on top of one another.

1 pound golden beets, peeled and finely diced

1 pound turnips, peeled and finely diced

1 pound carrots, peeled and finely diced

½ teaspoon salt

½ teaspoon freshly ground pepper

2 tablespoons olive oil

¼ cup balsamic vinegar

1. Preheat the oven to 450°F. Combine the beets, turnips, carrots, salt, and pepper in a large roasting pan. Drizzle the vegetables with the oil and toss to coat. Roast, stirring occasionally, until the vegetables are tender enough to be pierced with a knife, about 45 minutes.

2. Remove the pan from the oven; immediately add the vinegar, scraping up the browned bits from the bottom of the pan. Let cool 5 minutes, then serve.

Per serving (⅔ cup): 126 Cal, 5 g Fat, 1 g Sat Fat, 0 mg Chol, 325 mg Sod, 20 g Carb, 5 g Fib, 3 g Prot, 50 mg Calc. *POINTS: 2.*

FIVE-STAR TIP Potatoes, parsnips, celery root, and rutabaga are other root vegetables that would work well in this recipe. The salad can be refrigerated up to five days in an airtight container. Reheat in the microwave on High for 2 minutes or allow to come to room temperature before serving.

QUICK LIST

sun-dried tomatoes
romaine lettuce
mozzarella cheese
pepper
balsamic vinegar

Romaine, Mozzarella, and Sun-Dried Tomato Salad

MAKES 4 SERVINGS

Fresh basil adds delicacy while balsamic vinegar offers depth to this Roman-style salad. If you can find aged balsamic vinegar, try it in this recipe. Though a bit pricey, aged balsamic is prized for its complex, almost sweet flavor (and a little goes a long way). It's now available in many gourmet markets.

16 sun-dried tomato halves (not oil-packed)

2 cups thinly sliced romaine lettuce, rinsed (about 4 large leaves)

4 ounces fat-free mozzarella cheese, cut into ¼-inch pieces

½ teaspoon freshly ground pepper

2 tablespoons balsamic vinegar (preferably aged)

1. Combine the sun-dried tomatoes with enough water to cover in a small bowl; set aside until softened, about 10 minutes. Drain, pat dry with paper towels, and chop.

2. Combine the lettuce, mozzarella, sun-dried tomatoes, and pepper in a large bowl. Add the vinegar; toss gently to coat. Serve at once.

Per serving (1 cup): 71 Cal, 0 g Fat, 0 g Sat Fat, 3 mg Chol, 395 mg Sod, 8 g Carb, 2 g Fib, 10 g Prot, 427 mg Calc. **_POINTS: 1._**

FIVE-STAR TIP You can mix the greens, cheese, and sun-dried tomatoes earlier in the day. Keep them covered in the refrigerator, but to keep the greens from wilting, don't add the vinegar until you're ready to serve the salad.

barley
olive oil
cremini mushrooms
thyme
sherry vinegar

QUICK LIST

Barley and Wild Mushroom Salad

MAKES 4 SERVINGS

As we all know, mushrooms and barley make a great soup, so why shouldn't they make a great salad, too (especially with earthy cremini mushrooms, fresh thyme, and sherry vinegar in the mix)? For an elegant presentation, serve the salad in lettuce cups.

½ cup barley
1¾ cups water
1 tablespoon olive oil
½ pound cremini or white mushrooms, thinly sliced (3 cups)
2 teaspoons chopped thyme
½ teaspoon salt
½ teaspoon freshly ground pepper
2 tablespoons sherry vinegar

1. Combine the barley and water in a medium saucepan and bring to a boil. Reduce the heat and simmer, covered, until the barley is tender, about 30 minutes. Remove from the heat; let stand, covered, 10 minutes. Fluff with a fork and transfer to a medium bowl. Let cool 5 minutes.

2. Meanwhile, heat the oil in a large nonstick skillet over medium heat, then add the mushrooms. Cook, stirring, until softened, 5 minutes. Stir in the thyme, salt, and pepper, cook 1 minute; then add the vinegar and cook 10 seconds.

3. Spoon the mushroom mixture over the barley; toss gently to coat. Serve warm or at room temperature.

Per serving (¾ cup): 133 Cal, 4 g Fat, 1 g Sat Fat, 0 mg Chol, 295 mg Sod, 22 g Carb, 5 g Fib, 4 g Prot, 16 mg Calc. *POINTS: 2.*

FIVE-STAR TIP This salad can be stored in an airtight container in the refrigerator up to three days and serve chilled, making it a great portable item to take to a potluck or picnic.

QUICK LIST

garlic
shallots
kasha
bow tie pasta
cider vinegar

Kasha Varnishkes with Roasted Garlic and Shallots

MAKES 6 SERVINGS

This traditional Jewish pasta salad is served in New York delis alongside bowls of matzo ball soup. But it also makes a terrific side dish served with roast chicken, pork, or beef. You can cook the pasta up to two days in advance; rinse with cold water until cool, then refrigerate in a zip-close plastic bag. Kasha (roasted buckwheat groats), prized for its nutty flavor, is available in health-food stores and many supermarkets.

1 head garlic
5 large shallots, peeled
½ cup kasha
1 cup water
4 cups cooked bow ties
½ teaspoon salt
½ teaspoon freshly
   ground pepper
3 tablespoons cider vinegar

1. Preheat oven to 450°F. Remove any loose papery skin from the garlic, keeping the whole head intact. Cut off the top quarter of the head and discard. Spray a 12-inch square of foil with nonstick spray. Wrap the garlic and the shallots in the foil to form a packet. Roast the garlic and shallots until very soft, 50 minutes. Carefully unwrap and let cool.

2. Meanwhile, bring the kasha and water to a boil in a medium saucepan. Reduce the heat and simmer, covered, until the kasha is tender and the water is completely absorbed, about 10 minutes. Remove the pan from the heat. Let the kasha stand 5 minutes, then fluff with a fork and transfer to a large bowl.

3. Coarsely chop the roasted shallots. Squeeze the garlic cloves from their skins and coarsely chop.

4. Combine the kasha with the shallots, garlic, bow ties, salt, and pepper; drizzle with the cider vinegar and toss gently to coat.

Per serving (1 cup): 162 Cal, 1 g Fat, 0 g Sat Fat, 0 mg Chol, 199 mg Sod, 33 g Carb, 2 g Fib, 6 g Prot, 23 mg Calc. **POINTS: 3.**

FIVE-STAR TIP Bow ties are the traditional pasta shape for this dish, but you can use any medium-size pasta, like penne or ziti. The salad can be refrigerated in an airtight container up to two days. Return to room temperature before serving.

| dried chickpeas |
| feta cheese |
| tomato |
| black olives |
| lemon juice |

QUICK LIST

Greek Chickpea Salad

MAKES 6 SERVINGS

Chickpeas tossed with feta cheese, ripe tomato, olives, and lemon would be a typical lunch on the Cyclades, those heat-soaked, stark islands scattered across the Aegean, southeast of Athens. Adding marinated olives to the mix is a great way to perk up the salad's taste—without loading up on extra ingredients.

1 cup dried chickpeas (garbanzo beans), picked over, rinsed, and drained

4 cups water

1 ounce feta cheese, finely crumbled (¼ cup)

1 large tomato, chopped

16 pitted oil-cured marinated small black olives with herbs, finely chopped

½ teaspoon freshly ground pepper

2 tablespoons fresh lemon juice

1. Soak the chickpeas according to package directions.
2. Combine the soaked chickpeas and the water in a large saucepan and bring to a boil. Reduce the heat and simmer, covered, until tender, about 1 hour. Drain and rinse with cold water until cool.
3. Transfer the chickpeas to a large bowl; stir in the feta, tomato, olives, and pepper. Drizzle the top with the lemon juice and toss gently to coat.

Per serving (¾ cup): 169 Cal, 6 g Fat, 1 g Sat Fat, 4 mg Chol, 207 mg Sod, 22 g Carb, 6 g Fib, 7 g Prot, 60 mg Calc. **POINTS: 3.**

FIVE-STAR TIP For a simpler preparation, use canned chickpeas, but rinse them well to decrease their sodium content. Low-sodium canned chickpeas are available in health-food stores and some gourmet markets. You'll need 2 (15-ounce) cans chickpeas, rinsed and drained, for this recipe. Each can yields 1½ cups; use 2 cups, and reserve the remaining chickpeas, covered in the refrigerator, for another use.

Middle Eastern–Style
Lentil Salad

Middle Eastern–Style Lentil Salad

MAKES 4 SERVINGS

Consider trying this satisfying salad, spiked with a lemony sesame dressing, for a quick lunch or dinner. For a color and texture variation from the usual brown lentils, look for tiny green (French) lentils in the gourmet-food section of some supermarkets or in specialty-food stores. Sliced blood oranges make a lovely dessert with this entrée.

1¼ cups lentils, sorted and rinsed

4 cups water

6 ounces low-fat tofu, cut into ¼-inch pieces

4 scallions, thinly sliced

2 medium lemons

1 tablespoon tahini

½ teaspoon salt

½ teaspoon freshly ground pepper

1. Combine the lentils and water in a medium saucepan and bring to a boil. Reduce the heat and simmer, covered, until the lentils are tender but still hold their shape, about 13 minutes. Drain and rinse with cool water until warm.
2. Transfer the lentils to a large bowl; toss with the tofu and scallions.
3. To prepare the dressing, grate the zest of 1 lemon into a small bowl; add the juice of both lemons. Whisk in the tahini, salt, and pepper until well combined.
4. Pour the dressing over lentil mixture and toss gently to coat. Serve warm or at room temperature.

Per serving (1 cup): 238 Cal, 3 g Fat, 0 g Sat Fat, 0 mg Chol, 354 mg Sod, 38 g Carb, 10 g Fib, 18 g Prot, 68 mg Calc. **POINTS: 4.**

FIVE-STAR TIP You can use fat-free instead of low-fat extra-firm tofu, if desired. Tahini is a sesame-seed paste, available in health-food stores, Middle Eastern markets, and many supermarkets. The salad can be refrigerated in an airtight container up to four days.

Quinoa Salad

MAKES 4 SERVINGS

Quinoa (pronounced "keen-wah") was the staple grain of the ancient Inca culture and has made quite a comeback recently. The reason? Quinoa contains eight essential amino acids and is lower in carbohydrates than other grains. Like rice, quinoa cooks by absorbing all the liquid; it's done when the small sprout at one end forms a "halo" around the kernel. This sun-kissed salad includes tangerines, scallions, and fresh fennel. We suggest slicing the fennel with a box grater or a food processor fitted with the slicing blade.

½ cup quinoa

1 cup water

1 medium fennel bulb, very thinly sliced

4 tangerines, cut into sections

3 scallions, thinly sliced

¼ teaspoon freshly ground pepper

¼ cup low-fat vinaigrette dressing

1. Rinse the quinoa several times in cold water and drain. Combine the quinoa and the water in a medium saucepan and bring to a boil. Reduce the heat and simmer, covered, until the grains are tender and the water has been absorbed, about 12 minutes. Remove the pan from the heat. Let the quinoa stand, covered, 5 minutes.

2. Transfer the quinoa to a large bowl; add the fennel, tangerine sections, scallions, and pepper. Drizzle with the vinaigrette and toss gently to combine.

Per serving (¾ cup): 166 Cal, 4 g Fat, 0 g Sat Fat, 0 mg Chol, 131 mg Sod, 33 g Carb, 5 g Fib, 4 g Prot, 75 mg Calc. **POINTS: 3.**

FIVE-STAR TIP For an even easier salad, use 1 (11-ounce) can mandarin oranges, drained, instead of the tangerine sections. You will need ⅔ cup of the oranges, so just reserve the remaining oranges in the refrigerator for another use.

bulgur
red onion
parsley
mint
sour cherries

QUICK LIST

Snappy Tabbouleh

MAKES 4 SERVINGS

Tabbouleh is a classic Middle Eastern salad, made from bulgur—that is, wheat kernels that have been steamed, dried, and crushed. This simplified version includes the chopped parsley, mint, and onion of the traditional version but with a new twist: sour cherries! The salad can be stored, covered, in the refrigerator up to three days.

1½ cups boiling water
1 cup bulgur
1 small red onion, minced
¼ cup packed parsley, minced
¼ cup mint, minced
¾ cup jarred sour cherries, drained, chopped, with 3 tablespoons of juice reserved
½ teaspoon freshly ground pepper
¼ teaspoon salt

1. Pour the boiling water over the bulgur in a heatproof bowl; set aside until softened and all the liquid is absorbed, 15 minutes.
2. Fluff the bulgur with a fork; combine with the onion, parsley, mint, chopped sour cherries, pepper, and salt. Add the reserved cherry juice and toss to combine.

Per serving (1 cup): 147 Cal, 1 g Fat, 0 g Sat Fat, 0 mg Chol, 159 mg Sod, 33 g Carb, 8 g Fib, 5 g Prot, 38 mg Calc. **_POINTS: 2._**

dried white beans
water-packed tuna
sage
white-wine vinegar
extra-virgin olive oil

Tuna and White Bean Salad

MAKES 4 SERVINGS

Provence, that wide region of steep ocean bays and craggy mountains in southern France, inspires this salad with the flavors of fresh sage and a light vinaigrette. The dish can be prepared and refrigerated up to two days ahead; just allow it to return to room temperature before serving.

1 cup dried white beans, picked over, rinsed, and drained

4 cups water

1 (6-ounce) can water-packed tuna, drained

1 tablespoon minced sage

2 tablespoons white-wine vinegar

1 tablespoon extra-virgin olive oil

½ teaspoon salt

½ teaspoon freshly ground pepper

1. Soak the beans according to package directions.
2. Combine the soaked beans and the water in a large saucepan and bring to a boil. Reduce the heat and simmer, covered, until tender, about 45 minutes. Drain and rinse with cool water until cool.
3. Combine the beans, tuna, and sage in a large bowl; toss with the vinegar, oil, salt, and pepper to coat.

Per serving (¾ cup): 246 Cal, 5 g Fat, 1 g Sat Fat, 15 mg Chol, 432 mg Sod, 31 g Carb, 8 g Fib, 20 g Prot, 118 mg Calc. *POINTS: 5.*

FIVE-STAR TIP For an easier version, use 2 (15½-ounce) cans cannellini or great northern beans, rinsed and drained. This yields three cups of beans. You need 2½ cups beans for this recipe, so reserve the remaining beans, covered, in the refrigerator for another use.

5 RULES TO SPEEDY SUPERMARKET SHOPPING

Follow these handy tips and you'll get all of your marketing done in no time flat—leaving more time for the fun stuff!

1. **Think ahead.** It sounds obvious, but making a shopping list before you go to the store will make you stay focused on the task at hand. Organize the list into food groups (dairy, meats, produce, and so on) or coordinate the list with the layout of the store.

2. **Study the market.** Examine your supermarket with a critical eye and decide if it makes the grade. Does the market serve your needs quickly and efficiently (like accepting shopping lists by fax)? Are you satisfied with the customer service and quality of products? If not, you may need to shop around for a new store.

3. **Time it right.** Try not to shop during peak times (early weekday evenings and weekend afternoons), but go when the store is moderately busy so a full staff will be on duty. Late evenings and early Sunday mornings are usually the best times to shop.

4. **Shop solo.** It's easier to stay focused and save time when you shop alone. (If you can't, divide the shopping list with a partner: You pick up items in even aisles while your partner covers the odd aisles, then meet at the end of each aisle to compare notes.)

5. **Make a quick exit.** Study the checkout lines before rushing to join one. Look for a checkout person who seems attentive, fast, alert, and has someone to bag the groceries. (However, sometimes bagging your own groceries is faster and makes unpacking at home easier.)

Chapter 2

give me five!

5 ingredients, *5 POINTS* or less

QUICK LIST

chicken broth
lime juice
Thai red curry paste
eggs
cilantro

Thai Egg Drop Soup

MAKES 4 SERVINGS

This is not your ordinary take-out soup! The secret? A touch of Thai curry paste—a spicy blend of chiles, garlic, lemongrass, spices, and shrimp paste. You can find it in the ethnic-food section of most supermarkets. We use red curry paste here, but the green variety works equally well in this soul-warming brew.

1 (32-ounce) carton fat-free, low-sodium chicken broth
¼ cup fresh lime juice
¾ teaspoon Thai red curry paste
3 large eggs, lightly beaten
1 tablespoon chopped cilantro
⅛ teaspoon salt

1. Combine the chicken broth, lime juice, and curry paste in a large pot and bring to a boil. Reduce heat and simmer, 10 minutes.

2. Gradually add the eggs, whisking constantly to keep them from curdling. Cook, stirring constantly, 1 minute. Remove the soup from the heat, stir in the cilantro and salt, and serve at once.

Per serving (1 cup): 70 Cal, 4 g Fat, 1 g Sat Fat, 159 mg Chol, 747 mg Sod, 3 g Carb, 0 g Fib, 6 g Prot, 20 mg Calc. ***POINTS: 2.***

FIVE-STAR TIP A great twist on this recipe is to turn it into a Thai curried shrimp broth. Prepare the recipe as directed, omitting the eggs. Add 4 slices fresh ginger and 2 scallions, chopped, after the broth reaches a boil in Step 1. Instead of adding the eggs in Step 2, add ½ pound medium shrimp, peeled and deveined, and cook until the shrimp are opaque in the center, 3 to 4 minutes. Each 1-cup serving equals *1 POINT.*

Yukon Gold potatoes
leeks
onion
chicken broth
pepper

QUICK LIST

Leek and Golden Potato Soup

MAKES 6 SERVINGS

When you substitute all-purpose potatoes with buttery-tasting Yukon Golds, there's no need to add butter or oil to get a wonderfully rich-tasting soup. Once considered a specialty ingredient, these light-skinned potatoes can now be found in most supermarkets.

4 Yukon Gold potatoes, peeled and cut into ½-inch pieces

4 large leeks (about 2½ pounds), white and pale-green parts only, cleaned and chopped

1 large onion, chopped

5 cups fat-free, low-sodium chicken broth

¼ teaspoon freshly ground pepper

1. Combine the potatoes, leeks, onion, chicken broth, and pepper in a large pot and bring to a boil. Reduce the heat and simmer, covered, until the vegetables are tender, 22–25 minutes. Remove from the heat and let cool for 10 minutes.

2. Transfer the mixture to a blender and puree, working in batches, if necessary, to prevent overflow. Divide the soup among 6 bowls and serve.

Per serving (1⅓ cups): 141 Cal, 0 g Fat, 0 g Sat Fat, 0 mg Chol, 551 mg Sod, 32 g Carb, 3 g Fib, 4 g Prot, 49 mg Calc. ***POINTS: 2.***

FIVE-STAR TIP   To clean the leeks, trim the roots, leaving the root ends intact to hold the layers together. Slice them lengthwise, fan open the layers, and swish them in a large bowl of cool water. Let them stand a few minutes to allow the grit to fall to the bottom, then lift them out. This soup is terrific to make ahead and freeze. Just prepare the recipe as directed, quickly cool the soup over a bowl of ice, then freeze it in airtight containers up to two months.

QUICK LIST

Jamaican jerk seasoning
honey
soy sauce
olive oil
turkey breast

Caribbean-Style Roast Turkey Breast

MAKES 6 SERVINGS

If you buy a skinless boneless turkey breast, you'll enjoy the best part of the turkey without the hassle of roasting the whole bird. To catch that tropical taste, we marinate the breast in a simple mix of jerk seasoning, honey, soy sauce, and olive oil.

2 tablespoons Jamaican jerk seasoning
2 tablespoons honey
2 tablespoons reduced-sodium soy sauce
1 tablespoon olive oil
1 (1¾-pound) skinless boneless turkey-breast half

1. To prepare the marinade, combine the jerk seasoning, honey, soy sauce, and oil in a plastic zip-close bag; add the turkey. Squeeze out the air and seal the bag; turn to coat the turkey. Refrigerate, turning the bag occasionally, 3 hours or overnight.

2. Preheat the oven to 450°F. Place a wire rack in the center of a large roasting pan; spray with nonstick spray. Remove the turkey from the marinade and place on the wire rack. Roast until an instant-read thermometer inserted into the center of the breast registers 160°F, 40–45 minutes. Let stand 10 minutes before carving.

Per serving (about 3½ ounces): 150 Cal, 2 g Fat, 0 g Sat Fat, 72 mg Chol, 406 mg Sod, 5 g Carb, 0 g Fib, 26 g Prot, 11 mg Calc. **POINTS: 3.**

FIVE-STAR TIP   Use any leftover turkey to make a Caribbean-style pasta toss. Simply cut the turkey into cubes and toss with some cooked rotelle pasta, chopped fresh mango, pineapple, red onion, celery, and carrots. Make a dressing with fat-free mayonnaise, light sour cream, fresh lime juice, reduced-sodium soy sauce, and curry powder. Toss the dressing with the turkey and pasta mixture and serve over lettuce leaves.

maple syrup
garlic
thyme
ground cinnamon
quail

QUICK LIST

Maple-Marinated Quail

MAKES 4 SERVINGS

American quail are no relation to the similarly named European birds. Early colonists, noticing a resemblance between the two, aptly named the newly found bird quail. Today quail are primarily farm-raised and noted for their white meat and delicate flavor. They're a great choice for entertaining and can be found either fresh or frozen in better supermarkets and butcher shops. Try this entrée with some crisp roasted potatoes and a mesclun salad tossed with light balsamic vinaigrette.

3 tablespoons pure
maple syrup

2 cloves garlic, minced

2 teaspoons chopped
fresh thyme, or
½ teaspoon dried

¼ teaspoon ground
cinnamon

4 (3-ounce) quail

½ teaspoon salt

¼ teaspoon freshly
ground pepper

1. To prepare the marinade, combine the maple syrup, garlic, thyme, and cinnamon in a zip-close plastic bag; add the quail. Squeeze out the air and seal the bag; turn to coat the quail. Refrigerate, turning the bag occasionally, 1½ hours or overnight.

2. Preheat oven to 400°F. Spray a baking sheet with nonstick spray. Remove quail from the marinade, place on the baking sheet, and sprinkle with the salt and pepper. Roast until browned and the juices run clear when pricked with a knife, 25–30 minutes.

Per serving (1 quail): 140 Cal, 8 g Fat, 2 g Sat Fat, 51 mg Chol, 327 mg Sod, 3 g Carb, 0 g Fib, 13 g Prot, 14 mg Calc. *POINTS: 3.*

Turkey Fajita Rolls

MAKES 4 SERVINGS

Forget the tortillas! This south-of-the-border treat makes clever use of turkey cutlets to hold a scrumptious combo of roasted bell pepper strips and scallions. Add a salad of baby spinach leaves, garnish with fat-free sour cream, and you've got dinner.

1 red bell pepper, seeded and cut into thin strips

4 turkey cutlets (about 1 pound)

½ teaspoon Mexican seasoning spice blend

¼ teaspoon salt

4 scallions (green part only)

½ cup prepared salsa

1. Preheat oven to 450°F. Place the bell pepper strips on a baking sheet, lightly spray with nonstick spray. Roast until softened, 8–10 minutes. Set aside and cool.

2. Meanwhile, place each cutlet, with one long side facing you, on a work surface. Sprinkle the tops with the Mexican seasoning and salt; turn the cutlets over. Arrange one-fourth of the bell pepper strips and scallions across one short end of each cutlet and roll up to make 4 fajita rolls. (The ends of the scallion and bell peppers strips should extend out of each roll.) Secure the ends of the rolls with toothpicks.

3. Spray a large nonstick skillet with nonstick spray and set over medium-high heat. Add the fajita rolls and cook until browned, about 1 minute on each side. Wrap the handle of the skillet in foil. Transfer the skillet to the oven and roast until the rolls are cooked through, 7–10 minutes. Let stand 5 minutes before slicing.

Per serving (1 roll): 156 Cal, 1 g Fat, 0 g Sat Fat, 82 mg Chol, 363 mg Sod, 5 g Carb, 1 g Fib, 31 g Prot, 33 mg Calc. ***POINTS: 3.***

FIVE-STAR TIP   If the cutlets seem a bit thick, place them between two sheets of wax paper and pound with a meat mallet or small heavy saucepan until about ½-inch thick. For an easy weeknight meal, prepare the filling and assemble the fajita rolls the night before, then cover and refrigerate. When you get home from work, just brown them in the skillet and pop them in the oven to finish.

Turkey Fajita Rolls

QUICK LIST

pepper
eye-round roast
garlic
seasoned tomatoes
red wine

Beef Braised in Red Wine

MAKES 12 SERVINGS

Beef is well suited for long, gentle cooking—even the leaner cuts like this tender and juicy eye-round roast, which simmers in a luscious mixture of seasoned tomatoes and red wine. Serve the beef with roasted sliced sweet potatoes to soak up all the wonderful sauce.

1 teaspoon salt

½ teaspoon freshly ground pepper

1 (3-pound) beef eye-round roast, trimmed of all visible fat

4 cloves garlic, minced

1 can (28 ounces) Italian-seasoned crushed tomatoes

½ cup red wine

1. Sprinkle the salt and pepper all over the beef. Spray a large nonstick Dutch oven with nonstick spray and set over medium-high heat. Add the beef and brown on all sides, 2 minutes on each side. Transfer the beef to a large plate. Set aside.

2. Add the garlic to the same Dutch oven and cook until fragrant, 30 seconds. Stir in the tomatoes and wine; gently boil until the flavors blend, 5 minutes. Return the beef to the Dutch oven, reduce the heat, cover and simmer 1½ hours. Turn the beef over, cover, and simmer until fork-tender, 1½ hours longer.

3. Transfer the beef to a cutting board and cover to keep warm. Bring the wine mixture to a boil and cook, stirring occasionally, until it reduces by a third and thickens slightly, 10–12 minutes. Slice the beef and serve with the sauce.

Per serving (2 ounces beef with about ¼ cup sauce): 144 Cal, 7 g Fat, 3 g Sat Fat, 35 mg Chol, 429 mg Sod, 5 g Carb, 1 g Fib, 14 g Prot, 5 mg Calc. *POINTS: 3.*

FIVE-STAR TIP   If you have any leftover sauce, it freezes well in an airtight container. Try some on your favorite pasta or over sliced chicken breasts for a tasty last-minute meal.

tomato paste	QUICK LIST
chipotle en adobo	
lime	
ground cumin	
boneless sirloin steak	

Broiled Tex-Mex Steak

MAKES 6 SERVINGS

This cowboy-style steak gets its wild-west flavor from smoky chipotle chiles, lime, and ground cumin. It's also delicious prepared on the grill.

3 tablespoons tomato paste

1 chipotle en adobo plus 2 tablespoons adobo sauce

Juice and grated zest of 1 lime

1½ teaspoons ground cumin

1½ pounds boneless sirloin steak (about 1-inch thick), trimmed of all visible fat

1 teaspoon salt

1. To prepare the marinade, combine the tomato paste, chipotle and adobo sauce, lime juice and zest, and cumin in a zip-close plastic bag. Mash the mixture with a fork until smooth; add the steak. Squeeze out the air and seal the bag; turn to coat the steak. Refrigerate, turning the bag occasionally, 2 hours or overnight.

2. Spray the broiler pan with nonstick spray; preheat the broiler. Remove the steak from the marinade; sprinkle both sides with the salt. Broil the steak 4 inches from the heat until done to taste, 8–9 minutes on each side for medium-rare. Let stand 10 minutes before carving.

Per serving (about 3 ounces): 178 Cal, 7 g Fat, 3 g Sat Fat, 77 mg Chol, 473 mg Sod, 1 g Carb, 0 g Fib, 26 g Prot, 11 mg Calc. *POINTS: 4.*

FIVE-STAR TIP Use any leftover steak for a superspeedy weeknight meal. Thinly slice the steak and toss with packaged salad greens and your favorite fat-free vinaigrette. For some extra flavor, sprinkle the salad with a little grated Parmesan cheese and serve with a whole-grain roll.

Tenderloin of Beef with
Tarragon Butter
and Spicy Onion Tartlets

Tenderloin of Beef with Tarragon Butter

butter
tarragon
lemon zest
beef tenderloin
pepper

QUICK LIST

MAKES 4 SERVINGS

Beef tenderloin for only *4 POINTS*? Yes! Tenderloin medallions are naturally lean and need little fat to cook them to perfection. And because our herb butter is highly seasoned with fresh tarragon and grated lemon zest, you only need a teaspoon on each serving for luscious flavor. Tarragon has a distinctive licorice taste that complements the beef nicely in this recipe. But if you aren't a licorice fan, feel free to substitute minced chives or thyme. This dish makes a tasty combo with Spicy Onion Tartlets [see page 167].

4 teaspoons butter or
margarine, softened

2 teaspoons chopped
fresh tarragon or
½ teaspoon dried

1 teaspoon grated
lemon zest

¾ teaspoon salt

4 (3-ounce) center-cut
tenderloin medallions
(½-inch thick), trimmed
of all visible fat

⅛ teaspoon freshly
ground pepper

1. To prepare the tarragon butter, combine the butter, tarragon, lemon zest, and ¼ teaspoon of the salt in a small bowl. Set aside.

2. Spray a large nonstick skillet with nonstick spray and set over medium-high heat. Sprinkle the medallions with the remaining ½ teaspoon salt and the pepper. Cook the medallions until browned and done to taste, 3–4 minutes on each side for medium-rare. Top each medallion with about 1 teaspoon of the tarragon butter and serve at once.

Per serving (1 medallion with about 1 teaspoon butter): 168 Cal, 10 g Fat, 5 g Sat Fat, 63 mg Chol, 476 mg Sod, 0 g Carb, 0 g Fib, 18 g Prot, 8 mg Calc. *POINTS: 4.*

FIVE-STAR TIP The tarragon butter can be made up to two weeks ahead. Prepare the butter as directed, then wrap well in plastic wrap and freeze. Allow the butter to soften to room temperature before serving.

QUICK LIST

cumin seeds
fennel seeds
garlic powder
cayenne
eye-round toast

Spice-Crusted Roast Beef

MAKES 8 SERVINGS

This roast, rubbed with a gutsy spice blend, makes a great casual dinner served with steamed broccoli and mashed potatoes (with plenty of leftovers for sandwiches if you're serving a smaller crowd). To get a head start, make the spice mixture, omit the salt, press onto the beef, cover, and refrigerate overnight. Before roasting, sprinkle the beef with the salt and roast as directed.

1 tablespoon cumin seeds, lightly crushed

1 tablespoon fennel seeds, lightly crushed

1 teaspoon garlic powder

¼ teaspoon cayenne

1 teaspoon salt

1 (2-pound) eye-round roast, trimmed of all visible fat

1. Preheat the oven to 450°F. Line a roasting pan with foil; spray the foil with nonstick spray.

2. Combine the cumin, fennel, garlic powder, cayenne, and salt in a small bowl. Press the mixture all over the beef and place in a large roasting pan. Roast 45–55 minutes for medium-rare. Let stand 10 minutes before carving.

Per serving (3 ounces): 209 Cal, 12 g Fat, 5 g Sat Fat, 60 mg Chol, 342 mg Sod, 1 g Carb, 0 g Fib, 23 g Prot, 21 mg Calc. *POINTS: 5.*

extra-lean ground beef
dried currants
tomato paste
ground cumin
cinnamon

QUICK LIST

Moroccan Burgers

MAKES 4 SERVINGS

These simple, flavorful burgers are seasoned with a unique blend of tomato paste, dried currants, cumin, and cinnamon. They're great on their own with a tossed green salad or served in multigrain hamburger buns or toasted oat-bran English muffins with lettuce, tomato, and onion slices.

12 ounces extra-lean ground beef (7% or less fat)

2 tablespoons dried currants

1 tablespoon tomato paste

1 teaspoon ground cumin

½ teaspoon ground cinnamon

¾ teaspoon salt

¼ teaspoon freshly ground pepper

1. Combine the beef, currants, tomato paste, cumin, cinnamon, salt, and pepper; form the mixture into 4 (½-inch-thick) burgers.

2. Spray a large nonstick skillet with nonstick spray and set over medium heat. Add the burgers and cook, turning once, 3–4 minutes on each side for medium. Serve at once.

Per serving (1 burger): 111 Cal, 4 g Fat, 1 g Sat Fat, 37 mg Chol, 514 mg Sod, 5 g Carb, 1 g Fib, 14 g Prot, 12 mg Calc. ***POINTS: 2.***

FIVE-STAR TIP These burgers are great to make in bulk and freeze. Simply triple the recipe and form into 12 burgers. Wrap each burger in a double layer of plastic wrap, label them with the date, and freeze for up to three months. To serve, defrost in the refrigerator overnight and cook as directed.

QUICK LIST

seasoned white rice mix
bell peppers
extra-lean ground beef
vegetable juice
Parmesan cheese

Hearty Stuffed Bell Peppers

MAKES 4 SERVINGS

Stuffed peppers are usually filled with everything under the sun, often making it difficult to distinguish one ingredient from the other. Not in this recipe! A simple combination of preseasoned rice, lean ground beef, and Parmesan cheese works wonders in this satisfying stuffing. We prefer red bell peppers over green for their sweeter flavor, but you can combine red, yellow, green, and orange peppers for eye appeal. Serve with a shaved fennel and red onion salad or iceberg lettuce tossed with fat-free blue-cheese dressing.

⅓ cup seasoned white rice with tomato and basil (e.g., Uncle Ben's Tomato-Basil Rice)

4 small red bell peppers

10 ounces extra-lean ground beef (7% or less fat)

1½ cups 100% vegetable juice (e.g., V8 100% Vegetable Juice)

3 tablespoons grated Parmesan cheese

½ teaspoon salt

¼ teaspoon freshly ground pepper

1. Cook the rice according to package directions, omitting the butter or the vegetable oil. Cool 10 minutes.
2. Meanwhile, with a sharp knife, slice off the top inch of each bell pepper and remove the seeds. Set aside.
3. Combine the cooked rice, the ground beef, ¼ cup of the vegetable juice, the Parmesan, salt, and pepper in a medium bowl. Spoon the rice mixture—dividing it evenly—into the bell peppers.
4. Place the bell peppers in a 3-quart saucepan; pour the remaining 1¼ cups vegetable juice around the bell peppers and set the pan over medium-high heat. Bring the juice to a boil; reduce the heat, cover, and simmer until the bell peppers are tender and the beef is cooked through, 20–25 minutes. Place each bell pepper in a serving bowl and serve with the sauce.

Per serving (1 bell pepper with 5 tablespoons sauce): 186 Cal, 5 g Fat, 2 g Sat Fat, 35 mg Chol, 834 mg Sod, 20 g Carb, 2 g Fib, 16 g Prot, 107 mg Calc. **POINTS: 4.**

FIVE-STAR TIP If you want to bypass the seasoned rice, use 1 cup cooked white rice and bypass Step 1. This is a great make-ahead meal because the flavors of the bell peppers really develop as they sit in the sauce. Cool the peppers to room temperature, transfer with the sauce to an airtight container, and refrigerate overnight. To reheat, return the peppers and sauce to a 3-quart saucepan and simmer, covered, over medium-low heat until hot, 12 to 15 minutes.

Dijon mustard
garlic
rosemary
lemon zest
leg of lamb

QUICK LIST

Rosemary-Dijon Leg of Lamb

MAKES 6 SERVINGS

Leg of lamb is always an impressive party dish. For this recipe, we give it the classic treatment by marinating the meat with mustard, garlic, and fresh rosemary. For a prep-free side dish, roast some red potatoes along with the lamb on another oven rack.

4 tablespoons Dijon mustard

5 garlic cloves, minced

2 tablespoons chopped fresh rosemary, or
  2 teaspoons dried

Grated zest of 1 lemon

1 teaspoon salt

½ teaspoon freshly ground pepper

1 (5-pound) bone-in leg of lamb, trimmed of all visible fat

1. Preheat the oven to 375°F. Spray a large roasting pan with nonstick spray.

2. Combine the mustard, garlic, rosemary, lemon zest, salt, and pepper in a small bowl. Rub the mixture all over the lamb and place in the roasting pan. Roast until an instant-read thermometer inserted into the thickest part of the lamb registers 135°F, about 1 hour 20 minutes for medium-rare. Let stand 10 minutes before carving.

Per serving (3 ounces): 155 Cal, 10 g Fat, 4 g Sat Fat, 54 mg Chol, 214 mg Sod, 1 g Carb, 0 g Fib, 15 g Prot, 13 mg Calc. **POINTS: 4.**

QUICK LIST

scallions
soy sauce
lemon juice
cilantro
lamb chops

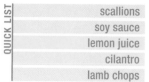

Broiled Lamb Chops with Soy-Scallion Relish

MAKES 4 SERVINGS

Lean and low in *POINTS*, quick-cooking lamb chops taste super when paired with Asian seasonings. Make this a satisfying meal by serving the chops with fragrant basmati rice and a speedy carrot-snow pea sauté.

2 scallions, finely chopped
1½ teaspoons reduced-sodium soy sauce
1 teaspoon fresh lemon juice
1 teaspoon chopped cilantro
4 (¼-pound) bone-in loin or rib-eye lamb chops, trimmed of all visible fat
½ teaspoon salt
⅛ teaspoon freshly ground pepper

1. Spray the broiler rack with nonstick spray; preheat the broiler.

2. Meanwhile, to prepare the relish, combine the scallions, soy sauce, lemon juice, and cilantro in a small bowl. Set aside.

3. Sprinkle the lamb with the salt and pepper. Broil 4 inches from the heat, until done to taste, 2–3 minutes on each side for medium. Serve at once with the relish.

Per serving (1 lamb chop with 2 teaspoons relish): 112 Cal, 5 g Fat, 2 g Sat Fat, 48 mg Chol, 410 mg Sod, 1 g Carb, 0 g Fib, 15 g Prot, 15 mg Calc. *POINTS: 3.*

FIVE-STAR TIP If you're not a fan of lamb, this dish is also terrific with boneless center-cut pork loin chops for the same number of *POINTS.*

dark brown sugar
Mexican seasoning
ground cumin
center-cut pork loin
barbecue sauce

QUICK LIST

Down-Home BBQ Pork

MAKES 6 SERVINGS

What makes this fabulous sweet-smoky barbecue so easy and tasty? The pork gets a double dose of seasoning—first rubbed with zesty spices, then basted with a tangy sauce while it cooks. And everything is done in the oven, so no fancy grilling is required.

2 tablespoons packed dark brown sugar

2 teaspoons Mexican seasoning spice blend

2 teaspoons ground cumin

¾ teaspoon salt

¼ teaspoon freshly ground pepper

1 (1½-pound) boneless center-cut pork loin, trimmed of all visible fat

⅓ cup fat-free barbecue sauce

1. Preheat oven to 400°F. Line a baking sheet with foil and spray the foil with nonstick spray.
2. Combine the brown sugar, Mexican seasoning, cumin, salt, and pepper in a small bowl. Rub the mixture all over the pork and place on the baking sheet.
3. Roast the pork 20 minutes. Brush the pork with half of the barbecue sauce; roast 10 minutes. Brush the pork with the remaining barbecue sauce and roast until the pork reaches an internal temperature of 160°F, 15–20 minutes longer. Let stand 10 minutes before carving.

Per serving (about 3 ounces): 213 Cal, 8 g Fat, 3 g Sat Fat, 67 mg Chol, 572 mg Sod, 10 g Carb, 0 g Fib, 24 g Prot, 31 mg Calc. **POINTS: 5.**

FIVE-STAR TIP Turn leftover barbecue pork into easy burritos: Slice or chop the pork and reheat in the microwave. Spoon some pork onto a warm flour tortilla, top with cooked rice, prepared salsa, fat-free cheddar cheese, and pickled jalapeños. Roll up and enjoy.

QUICK LIST

cracked pepper
garlic powder
pork chops
arugula
red-wine vinaigrette

Cracked-Pepper Pork Chops

MAKES 4 SERVINGS

These slightly spicy, pungent chops are flash-cooked on a grill pan, then served piping hot over an arugula salad. Just add a side of freshly steamed corn on the cob or our zippy Paprikash Noodles [see page 61] for a great weeknight meal.

1 tablespoon cracked black pepper

1 teaspoon garlic powder

¾ teaspoon salt

4 (¼-pound) boneless center-cut pork chops, trimmed of all visible fat

1 large bunch arugula, (about 4 cups)

3 tablespoons fat-free red-wine vinaigrette

1. Combine the cracked pepper, garlic powder, and salt in a small bowl. Press the mixture onto both sides of the pork chops; set aside.

2. Spray a nonstick ridged grill pan with nonstick spray and set over medium-high heat. Grill the pork until browned and cooked through, turning once, 6–8 minutes. Transfer the pork to a plate and keep warm.

3. Combine the arugula and vinaigrette in a large bowl; toss well to coat. Divide the arugula among 4 plates and top each plate with 1 pork chop. Serve at once.

Per serving (1 pork chop with 1 cup arugula): 172 Cal, 6 g Fat, 2 g Sat Fat, 59 mg Chol, 597 mg Sod, 6 g Carb, 1 g Fib, 22 g Prot, 61 mg Calc. *POINTS: 4.*

FIVE-STAR TIP While you can easily find cracked pepper in jars in the supermarket's spice aisle, nothing compares to the flavor of freshly cracked pepper. Use a mortar and pestle, rolling pin, mallet, or even the side of an unopened can to coarsely crush whole black peppercorns on a work surface.

**Cracked-Pepper Pork Chops
and Paprikash Noodles**

QUICK LIST

light butter
shallots
shiitake mushrooms
dry sherry
veal loin chops

Grilled Veal Chops with Shiitake Mushrooms

MAKES 4 SERVINGS

Veal chops have a delicate, sweet flavor that balances wonderfully with mushrooms. The two are paired together quite often—but unfortunately swimming in a heavy cream sauce. We've managed to lighten the dish by grilling the veal rather than sautéing it in butter, skipping the cream, and cooking the mushrooms with shallots and a splash of sherry. Feel free to substitute skinless boneless chicken breast or center-cut loin pork chops.

2 teaspoons light butter

2 shallots, minced

12 ounces shiitake mushrooms, thinly sliced

½ teaspoon salt

¼ teaspoon freshly ground pepper

⅓ cup dry sherry

4 (6-ounce) bone-in veal loin chops (about ½-inch thick), trimmed of all visible fat

1. To prepare the mushrooms, melt the butter in a nonstick skillet over medium-high heat, then add the shallots. Cook, stirring occasionally, until the shallots start to soften, 2–3 minutes. Add the mushrooms, ¼ teaspoon of the salt, and ⅛ teaspoon of the pepper. Cook until the mushrooms soften, 5–6 minutes. Add the sherry and cook until most of the liquid has evaporated, 1–2 minutes. Remove from the heat and keep warm.

2. Spray a nonstick ridged grill pan with nonstick spray and set over medium-high heat. Sprinkle the veal with the remaining ¼ teaspoon salt and ⅛ teaspoon pepper. Grill the veal until done to taste, 3–4 minutes on each side for medium-rare. Serve with the mushrooms.

Per serving (1 veal chop with 6 tablespoons mushrooms): 216 Cal, 8 g Fat, 3 g Sat Fat, 95 mg Chol, 384 mg Sod, 7 g Carb, 1 g Fib, 27 g Prot, 28 mg Calc. *POINTS: 5.*

FIVE-STAR TIP This recipe is a good opportunity to use the wide assortment of exotic mushrooms that are now readily available at the supermarket. Shiitake, cremini, and portobello mushrooms are a great combination to try.

precut fresh vegetables	QUICK LIST
olive oil	
crushed red pepper	
lemon zest	
orange zest	

Citrus-Roasted Vegetables

MAKES 6 SERVINGS

What's *another* great thing about vegetables? You can pile them on your plate and not load up on *POINTS!* Better yet, to keep this recipe at five ingredients and super convenient, we use a fresh vegetable blend of precut broccoli, cauliflower, and carrots—readily available in the supermarket produce aisle.

2 (12-ounce) bags assorted precut fresh vegetables (broccoli, cauliflower, and carrots)

1½ tablespoons olive oil

¼ teaspoon crushed red pepper

¾ teaspoon salt

1 teaspoon grated lemon zest

1 teaspoon grated orange zest

1. Preheat oven to 450°F. Spray a large jelly-roll pan with nonstick spray; set aside.

2. Combine the vegetables, oil, red pepper, and salt in a large bowl; toss well. Transfer the vegetable mixture to the jelly-roll pan; roast until the vegetables are tender, 20–22 minutes.

3. Return the vegetables to the same bowl; add the lemon zest and orange zest and toss well to coat. Serve at once.

Per serving (generous ¾ cup): 65 Cal, 4 g Fat, 1 g Sat Fat, 0 mg Chol, 319 mg Sod, 7 g Carb, 3 g Fib, 2 g Prot, 35 mg Calc. *POINTS: 1.*

FIVE-STAR TIP   Packaged vegetable blends are available in a number of different varieties (such as broccoli, baby carrots, snap peas, and celery), so feel free to experiment with different combinations to compliment various meals. To save time, make this dish the night before and refrigerate overnight. Add it chilled to your favorite salad mix or microwave on High until heated through, 1 to 2 minutes.

**Tofu Stir-fry
with Snow Peas**

hoisin sauce
Asian sesame oil
low-fat tofu
snow peas
fresh ginger

QUICK LIST

Tofu Stir-fry with Snow Peas

MAKES 4 SERVINGS

Silky tofu and crunchy snow peas, flash-cooked with sweet-and-spicy hoisin sauce, make an outstanding last-minute meal. To vary this recipe, use a 12-ounce bag of fresh vegetables-for-stir-fry blend instead of the snow peas.

2½ tablespoons hoisin sauce

1 tablespoon water

2 teaspoons Asian (dark) sesame oil

12 ounces low-fat firm tofu, cut into ½-inch cubes

½ pound fresh snow peas, trimmed

1 tablespoon minced peeled fresh ginger

1. Combine the hoisin sauce and water in a small bowl; set aside.

2. Heat 1 teaspoon of the sesame oil in a large nonstick skillet over medium-high heat, then add the tofu. Cook, stirring, until browned, 3–4 minutes. Transfer the tofu to a plate; set aside.

3. Heat the remaining 1 teaspoon sesame oil in the same skillet. Add the snow peas and ginger and cook 2 minutes. Add the tofu and cook 1 minute. Stir in the hoisin mixture and cook until heated through; 30 seconds longer. Serve at once.

Per serving (1 cup): 97 Cal, 3 g Fat, 1 g Sat Fat, 0 mg Chol, 237 mg Sod, 9 g Carb, 2 g Fib, 8 g Prot, 57 mg Calc. **POINTS: 2.**

FIVE-STAR TIP If you gently press the tofu between layers of paper towels to remove excess moisture, it will brown more readily in the skillet. Serve this stir-fry with quick-cooking white or brown rice for a complete meal.

QUICK LIST

Swiss chard
Asian sesame oil
soy sauce
toasted sesame seeds

Sesame Swiss Chard

MAKES 4 SERVINGS

Swiss chard is a leafy-green member of the beet family. Known for its tender leaves and crisp stalks, chard is a good source of iron as well as vitamins A and C. For a change from the ordinary, look for ruby chard, which has bright red stalks and green-tinged red leaves, at the farmers' market or in the produce section of some supermarkets. We precook the chard with the water clinging to its leaves from rinsing—a trick that cuts down on the fat usually needed for cooking.

2 bunches Swiss chard (about 2 pounds), rinsed and large stalks removed

1 teaspoon Asian (dark) sesame oil

4 teaspoons reduced-sodium soy sauce

1½ teaspoons toasted sesame seeds

1. Heat a large nonstick Dutch oven over medium-high heat. Add the chard, one-third at a time, stirring, until each batch wilts, 3–4 minutes. Transfer the chard to a colander; press the chard with a wooden spoon to extract as much liquid as possible.

2. Heat the oil in the same Dutch oven over medium-high heat. Add the chard and soy sauce. Cook, stirring, until tender and heated through, 2–3 minutes. Remove from the heat, then stir in the sesame seeds.

Per serving (generous ⅓ cup): 57 Cal, 2 g Fat, 0 g Sat Fat, 0 mg Chol, 542 mg Sod, 9 g Carb, 4 g Fib, 4 g Prot, 111 mg Calc. **POINTS: 1.**

FIVE-STAR TIP   To make this a complete meal, serve the chard with some stir-fried shrimp and steamed brown rice.

Pan-Roasted Brussels Sprouts with Fingerling Potatoes

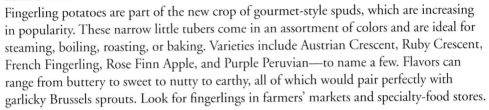

QUICK LIST

fingerling potatoes
olive oil
Brussels sprouts
garlic
pepper

MAKES 6 SERVINGS

Fingerling potatoes are part of the new crop of gourmet-style spuds, which are increasing in popularity. These narrow little tubers come in an assortment of colors and are ideal for steaming, boiling, roasting, or baking. Varieties include Austrian Crescent, Ruby Crescent, French Fingerling, Rose Finn Apple, and Purple Peruvian—to name a few. Flavors can range from buttery to sweet to nutty to earthy, all of which would pair perfectly with garlicky Brussels sprouts. Look for fingerlings in farmers' markets and specialty-food stores.

¾ pound fingerling potatoes, rinsed and cut into ¼-inch-thick slices

2 tablespoons olive oil

1½ pounds Brussels sprouts, trimmed and halved

5 cloves garlic, thinly sliced

¾ teaspoon salt

¼ teaspoon freshly ground pepper

1. Combine the potatoes with enough cold water to cover by 2 inches in a medium saucepan and bring to a boil. Boil 1 minute. Remove the potatoes from the heat and let stand in the cooking liquid until partially cooked, 5 minutes. Drain and set aside.

2. Meanwhile, heat the oil in a large nonstick skillet over medium heat, then add the Brussels sprouts. Cook until bright green, 6–8 minutes. Add the garlic and cook until the Brussels sprouts begin to brown, 3–4 minutes. Stir in the potatoes, salt, and pepper and cook until the vegetables are tender, 5–7 minutes longer. Serve warm or at room temperature.

Per serving (1 cup): 142 Cal, 5 g Fat, 1 g Sat Fat, 0 mg Chol, 321 mg Sod, 23 g Carb, 4 g Fib, 4 g Prot, 54 mg Calc. ***POINTS: 2.***

FIVE-STAR TIP You can also use small red potatoes in this recipe instead of the fingerlings. To make this flavorful side dish a complete meal, serve it with 6 (6-ounce) broiled flounder fillets seasoned with salt, pepper, and fresh lemon juice for *6 POINTS* a serving.

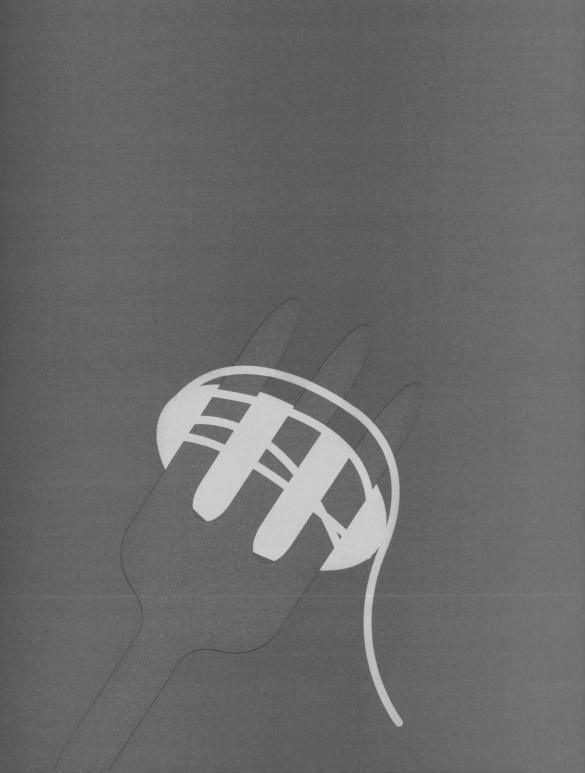

Chapter 3

pasta! pasta! pasta!

with an array of flavors from around the world

QUICK LIST

chicken broth
frozen vegetables
shiitake mushrooms
thyme
egg noodles

Shiitake-Vegetable Noodle Soup

MAKES 4 SERVINGS

Shiitake mushrooms add rich, woodsy flavor to our favorite comfort classic—chicken noodle soup. We also add assorted precut frozen veggies for a nutrient boost; they're available in a wide variety, so substitute another combo, if desired. Cooking the noodles separately and then adding them to the soup just before serving prevents them from becoming mushy. For a heartier version (and an extra *1 POINT* per serving) add 4 ounces cooked diced chicken before serving.

1 (32-ounce) carton low-sodium chicken broth

2 cups corn, broccoli, and red bell pepper frozen vegetable blend

1 (3½-ounce) package shiitake mushrooms, stems removed, sliced

Pinch dried thyme

1¼ cups broad cholesterol-free egg noodles

1. Bring the broth to a boil in a medium saucepan; add the frozen vegetables, mushrooms, and thyme. Reduce the heat and simmer until the vegetables are tender, 4–5 minutes.

2. Meanwhile, cook the noodles according to package directions. Drain and add to the soup. Serve at once.

Per serving (1 cup plus 2 tablespoons): 249 Cal, 3 g Fat, 1 g Sat Fat, 5 mg Chol, 161 mg Sod, 50 g Carb, 7 g Fib, 12 g Prot, 43 mg Calc. *POINTS: 4.*

FIVE-STAR TIP   Substitute white mushrooms for the shiitake, if desired. You may also use regular wide egg noodles for the same number of *POINTS* per serving.

chicken broth
serrano pepper or Thai chile
garlic
star anise pod
rice-stick noodle

QUICK LIST

Asian-Spiced Noodle Soup

MAKES 4 SERVINGS

This one-pot soup, spiced with a heady mix of garlic, chiles, and star anise, is ready in a matter of minutes. Light and fragrant, it makes a wonderful first course as part of a Chinese menu. Or, if you prefer a main-dish soup for the same number of *POINTS,* stir in 4 ounces thawed frozen cooked shrimp with the noodles.

1 (32-ounce) box low-sodium chicken broth
1 teaspoon finely chopped serrano pepper or Thai chile (wear gloves to prevent irritation)
1 large clove garlic, thinly sliced
½ star anise pod
2 ounces rice-stick noodles

Combine the broth, serrano pepper, garlic, and star anise in a saucepan and bring to a boil. Reduce the heat; add the noodles and cook until the noodles are just tender, 2–3 minutes. Serve at once.

Per serving (about 1 cup): 92 Cal, 2 g Fat, 1 g Sat Fat, 5 mg Chol, 130 mg Sod, 14 g Carb, 0 g Fib, 5 g Prot, 27 mg Calc. *POINTS: 2.*

QUICK LIST

asparagus
olive oil
garlic
lemon
linguine

Linguine with Roasted Asparagus and Lemon

MAKES 4 SERVINGS

Roasting intensifies the flavor of many vegetables, especially asparagus—concentrating its delicious sweetness. Contrary to popular belief, pencil-thin asparagus is no more tender than the thicker jumbo variety. Either works beautifully in this recipe; just increase or decrease the roasting time accordingly.

1¼ pounds asparagus, trimmed
1 tablespoon olive oil
3 cloves garlic, crushed through a press
Juice and grated zest of 1 lemon
½ teaspoon salt
⅛ teaspoon freshly ground pepper
½ pound linguine

1. Preheat the oven to 425°F. Spray a broiler pan or large jelly-roll pan with nonstick spray. Place the asparagus on the pan and lightly spray with nonstick spray. Roast until lightly charred in spots and tender, 12–14 minutes. When cool enough to handle, cut into 1½-inch pieces.
2. Meanwhile, combine the oil and garlic in a microwavable cup; microwave on High until just warm and fragrant, 30–40 seconds. Stir the lemon juice and zest, salt, and pepper into the garlic-oil mixture.
3. Cook the linguine according to package directions. Drain, reserving ¼ cup of the cooking liquid. Toss the linguine, asparagus, and garlic-oil mixture in a large serving bowl, adding enough of the reserved liquid to evenly moisten. Serve at once.

Per serving (scant 1¼ cups): 276 Cal, 5 g Fat, 1 g Sat Fat, 0 mg Chol, 301 mg Sod, 50 g Carb, 4 g Fib, 10 g Prot, 31 mg Calc. **POINTS: 5.**

FIVE-STAR TIP When selecting asparagus, look for bright green stalks with closed compact, firm tips. If the tips are slightly wilted, refresh them by briefly soaking the stalks in cold water.

onion
hot paprika
light cream cheese
yogurt
fettuccini

QUICK LIST

Paprikash Noodles

MAKES 4 SERVINGS

Creamy whole-milk yogurt contains far less fat than cream or half-in-half and is less tart than low-fat yogurt. It also makes a great substitute for the sour cream traditionally used in paprikash. The trick to cooking with yogurt: Don't be tempted to heat it over a flame, because it will break apart. Fettuccine is often paired with rich sauces, and this dish is no exception. So we serve it in smaller portions, making it a perfect side dish for our zesty Cracked-Pepper Pork Chops [see page 48] or roast chicken and a crisp green salad.

⅓ cup minced onion

1 teaspoon hot paprika (preferably Hungarian)

¾ teaspoon salt

1 ounce light cream cheese (Neufchâtel)

¾ cup plain whole-milk yogurt

½ pound fettuccini

1. To prepare the sauce, spray a small saucepan with nonstick spray and set over medium heat. Add the onion and cook until softened, 3–4 minutes. Add the paprika and ½ teaspoon of the salt; cook, stirring, until just fragrant, 30 seconds. Remove the pan from the heat, and let the onion mixture cool a few minutes. Stir in the cream cheese until melted and smooth. Then stir in the yogurt and the remaining ¼ teaspoon salt until blended.

2. Meanwhile, cook the fettuccini according to package directions. Drain and toss with sauce in a large serving bowl.

Per serving (generous ¾ cup): 207 Cal, 5 g Fat, 2 g Sat Fat, 11 mg Chol, 588 mg Sod, 35 g Carb, 2 g Fib, 8 g Prot, 65 mg Calc. **_POINTS: 4._**

QUICK LIST

plum tomatoes
cavatappi or trumpetti
extra-virgin olive oil
kalamata olives
basil

Pasta with Roasted Tomatoes and Olives

MAKES 4 SERVINGS

Roasting is a terrific way to bring out the intense sweetness of fresh tomatoes, even if they're not fully ripe. Fresh basil adds a hint of licorice and kalamata olives offer a rich, fruity undertone to this Mediterranean-style sauce. If you want to cheat and add another ingredient, sprinkle the pasta with 2 ounces crumbled reduced-fat feta cheese (and add *1 POINT* per serving).

8 medium plum tomatoes (about 1½ pounds)

½ pound cavatappi or trumpetti

5 teaspoons extra-virgin olive oil

15 pitted kalamata olives in brine, sliced (about ¼ cup) + 1 teaspoon brine

½ teaspoon salt

¼ teaspoon freshly ground pepper

¼ cup packed basil leaves, thinly sliced

1. Preheat the oven to 325°F. Line a jelly-roll pan with parchment. Halve the tomatoes lengthwise and place cut-side up in the pan. Roast until the tomatoes are very tender, 1 hour 15 minutes.

2. Meanwhile, cook the pasta according to package directions. Drain, reserving 2 tablespoons of the cooking liquid. Rinse the pasta with cool water until just warm.

3. Puree 6 of the tomato halves with the oil, the reserved cooking liquid, the 1 teaspoon brine from the olives, the salt, and pepper in a blender. Halve the remaining tomato halves lengthwise; transfer to a large serving bowl and add the pasta, basil, and olives. Pour the pureed tomatoes over the top and toss lightly to coat.

Per serving (1⅓ cups): 301 Cal, 10 g Fat, 1 g Sat Fat, 0 mg Chol, 492 mg Sod, 48 g Carb, 4 g Fib, 8 g Prot, 11 mg Calc. *POINTS: 6.*

FIVE-STAR TIP If you have an enamel-coated broiler pan, it's perfect for roasting acidic vegetables like tomatoes because the coating won't react to the acids (unlike aluminum pans, which, if not lined with parchment, will give baked tomatoes a metallic taste).

Pasta with Roasted
Tomatoes and Olives

Cavatappi with Roasted Red Onions and Arugula

MAKES 4 SERVINGS

Oven-roasted sweet red onions, peppery arugula, and a touch of broth (versus a dousing of oil) give this simple pasta toss sophisticated taste. You can substitute watercress or fresh spinach for the greens, or whole-wheat penne or fusilli for the cavatappi, if desired.

1 large red onion, cut into chunks

4 teaspoons extra-virgin olive oil

½ teaspoon salt

⅔ cup low-sodium chicken broth

½ pound cavatappi (ridged spiral-shaped pasta)

1 large bunch arugula, coarsely chopped

¼ teaspoon freshly ground pepper

1. Preheat the oven to 450°F.
2. Combine the onion with 1 teaspoon of the oil and ¼ teaspoon of the salt in a broiler pan or jelly-roll pan. Cover the pan tightly with foil and roast the onions until softened and brown in spots, 12 minutes. Remove the foil, stir the onions, and roast, uncovered, until the onions caramelize, 6–9 minutes more. Transfer the onions to a large serving bowl.
3. Add the broth to the same broiler pan and set over medium heat. Bring to a low boil and cook, scraping up the browned bits from the bottom of the pan, until reduced to ½ cup, 1–2 minutes.
4. Meanwhile, cook the cavatappi according to package directions. Drain and toss with the onions, broth mixture, arugula, oil, the remaining ¼ teaspoon salt, and the pepper. Serve at once.

Per serving (1½ cups): 269 Cal, 6 g Fat, 1 g Sat Fat, 1 mg Chol, 320 mg Sod, 46 g Carb, 3 g Fib, 9 g Prot, 73 mg Calc. **POINTS: 5.**

Orecchiette with Garlic, Red Pepper, and Broccoli Rabe

broccoli rabe
garlic oil
crushed red pepper
orecchiette
salt

QUICK LIST

MAKES 6 SERVINGS

Broccoli rabe, an assertive leafy green with a peppery-sharp flavor, is typically paired with this small saucer-shaped pasta in southern Italy. If you're looking for milder flavor, use regular broccoli and reduce the crushed red pepper to ¼ teaspoon.

1 large bunch broccoli rabe, trimmed
1 tablespoon garlic oil
½ teaspoon crushed red pepper
½ teaspoon salt
½ pound orecchiette

1. Put the broccoli rabe in a steamer basket; set in a saucepan over 1 inch boiling water. Cover tightly and steam until tender, 6 minutes. Set ¼ cup of the cooking liquid aside. Cool the broccoli rabe slightly and coarsely chop.
2. Heat the oil in a large nonstick skillet over medium heat, then add the crushed red pepper. Cook until the crushed red pepper darkens slightly, about 30 seconds. Add the broccoli rabe and salt and cook until heated through, 2–3 minutes.
3. Meanwhile, cook the orecchiette according to package directions. Drain and toss with the broccoli rabe mixture and the reserved cooking liquid in a large serving bowl.

Per serving (1½ cups): 183 Cal, 3 g Fat, 0 g Sat Fat, 0 mg Chol, 205 mg Sod, 33 g Carb, 1 g Fib, 7 g Prot, 21 mg Calc. **POINTS: 4.**

FIVE-STAR TIP   Cook the remaining ½ pound orecchiette separately for another meal later in the week. Cook according to package directions, then drain and rinse with cold water, shaking vigorously to get rid of any excess water. Transfer the pasta to a large bowl and toss with 1½ teaspoons vegetable oil. Cover and refrigerate up to three days. To reheat, cook the pasta in boiling water until just heated, about a minute; drain and toss with desired sauce.

Gemelli with
Bell Peppers and
Tomatillo

Gemelli with Bell Peppers and Tomatillo

red bell peppers
fresh corn
gemelli
roasted tomatillo salsa
goat cheese

QUICK LIST

MAKES 4 SERVINGS

This Mexicali-style dish features gemelli (medium-size pasta that resembles two pieces of spaghetti twisted together), roasted bell peppers, and fresh corn. When the hot cooked pasta and veggies are tossed with the salsa and cheese, they releases the tangy, citruslike flavor of the tomatillos and melt the cheese, creating a fabulous sauce. For best results, have the salsa and cheese at room temperature.

2 large red bell peppers

3 ears of corn, kernels removed (about 2 cups)

½ pound gemelli

½ cup roasted tomatillo salsa or salsa verde

3 ounces goat cheese, crumbled

½ teaspoon salt

1. Preheat the broiler. Line the broiler pan with foil; place the bell peppers on the broiler pan. Broil 4 inches from the heat, turning occasionally with tongs, until evenly charred, 13–16 minutes. Remove the peppers from the broiler, then wrap in the foil and let steam 20 minutes. When cool enough to handle, peel, core, and seed the peppers and cut them into ½-inch-wide strips.
2. Heat a 12-inch nonstick skillet over medium-high heat. Add the corn and cook until lightly charred in spots, 2 minutes; transfer to a large serving bowl.
3. Meanwhile, cook the gemelli according to package directions. Drain, reserving ½ cup of the cooking liquid.
4. Toss the gemelli, salsa, peppers, goat cheese, salt, and enough of the reserved liquid with the corn until the cheese is melted and the sauce is creamy. Serve at once.

Per serving (1½ cups): 379 Cal, 9 g Fat, 5 g Sat Fat, 17 mg Chol, 511 mg Sod, 64 g Carb, 6 g Fib, 15 g Prot, 84 mg Calc. **POINTS: 8.**

FIVE-STAR TIP   Any variety of salsa works well in this recipe, so you can control the amount of heat by choosing mild, medium, or hot. The bell peppers and corn can be roasted and refrigerated in separate zip-close plastic bags up to two days ahead.

QUICK LIST

medium shells
canned chickpeas
red-wine vinegar
garlic oil
hot pepper

Zesty Chickpeas and Shells

MAKES 4 SERVINGS

If you're looking for an easy, beat-the-heat entrée, this speedy pasta with no-cook dressing is a terrific choice. It also makes a great side dish served with grilled chicken, fish, or beef.

2¾ cups medium shells

1 (15½-ounce) can chickpeas (garbanzo beans), rinsed and drained

2 tablespoons red-wine vinegar

4 teaspoons garlic oil or extra-virgin olive oil

1 tablespoon water

½ teaspoon salt

1 red Fresno or jalapeño pepper, seeded and minced (wear gloves to prevent irritation)

1. Cook the shells according to package directions. Drain and rinse with cool water until just warm.

2. Meanwhile, pulse ½ cup of the chickpeas, the vinegar, oil, water, and salt in a blender until almost smooth. Scrape into a large serving bowl; stir in the pepper. Add the shells and the remaining chickpeas and toss to coat.

Per serving (1 cup plus 1 tablespoon): 384 Cal, 8 g Fat, 1 g Sat Fat, 0 mg Chol, 388 mg Sod, 68 g Carb, 5 g Fib, 13 g Prot, 38 mg Calc. **POINTS: 8.**

FIVE-STAR TIP   You can refrigerate the dressing and the whole chickpeas in separate airtight containers and the cooked shells in a large zip-close plastic bag up to two days. To serve, microwave the dressing in a microwavable bowl until barely warm, 20 to 40 seconds. Rinse the shells under hot water until room temperature. Drain and toss with the dressing, whole chickpeas, and minced pepper.

eggplant
diced tomatoes with garlic
capers
mostaccioli
feta cheese

QUICK LIST

Mostaccioli with Eggplant and Feta Cheese

MAKES 4 SERVINGS

Cooking eggplant need not require a lot of fat. The trick is to steam it with a bit of water in a tightly covered skillet over low heat. If the water evaporates and the eggplant begins to stick, just add another 1 to 2 tablespoons water. Serve this Greek-style pasta alongside a crisp romaine lettuce salad with sliced cucumbers and scallions.

1 small eggplant, peeled and cut into 1-inch cubes (about ¾ pound)

¼ cup water

1 (14½-ounce) can diced tomatoes with roasted garlic

1 tablespoon capers, drained

½ teaspoon salt

¼ teaspoon freshly ground pepper

½ pound mostaccioli or ziti

2 ounces reduced-fat feta cheese, crumbled (about ½ cup)

1. To prepare the sauce, spray a 12-inch nonstick skillet with nonstick spray and set over medium-low heat. Add the eggplant and water, cover, and cook until the eggplant has softened, 11–13 minutes.

2. Increase the heat; add the tomatoes, capers, salt, and pepper and bring to a low boil. Partially cover the skillet and cook until the sauce thickens and the eggplant is very tender, 10–13 minutes.

3. Meanwhile, cook the mostaccioli according to package directions. Drain and toss with the sauce in a large serving bowl. Sprinkle with the feta and serve.

Per serving (1¾ cups): 289 Cal, 3 g Fat, 2 g Sat Fat, 5 mg Chol, 1,044 mg Sod, 54 g Carb, 4 g Fib, 12 g Prot, 108 mg Calc. **_POINTS: 5._**

FIVE-STAR TIP   We like to use nonpareil capers, which are the smallest variety, for this recipe. If you can only find the larger capers, just chop them before adding to the sauce. You can also prepare the sauce and refrigerate it in an airtight container up to three days ahead. To serve, transfer the sauce to a medium saucepan, cover, and cook over medium-low heat, stirring occasionally, until hot. Then toss with the mostaccioli as directed.

QUICK LIST

Thai satay peanut sauce
almond milk
fresh ginger
somen noodles
scallions

Thai-Style Peanut Noodles

MAKES 4 SERVINGS

Satay is a dish usually associated with grilled skewers of meat or poultry served with a spicy peanut sauce. But we've discovered that prepared satay sauce, now widely available in the ethnic-food section of the supermarket, also makes a delicious dressing for cold somen noodles. The addition of nondairy almond milk keeps the peanut dressing low in fat. Look for this vitamin-enriched, cholesterol-free beverage in the gourmet or natural-food section of your supermarket or health-food store.

¼ cup Thai satay peanut sauce

⅓ cup almond milk or low-fat (2%) milk

1 teaspoon peeled and grated fresh ginger

½ teaspoon salt

⅛ teaspoon freshly ground pepper

½ pound somen noodles

¼ cup very thinly sliced scallions

1. To prepare the dressing, puree the satay sauce, almond milk, ginger, salt, and pepper in a blender.
2. Cook the noodles according to package directions. Drain and rinse with cool water until cool. Toss the noodles with the dressing and scallions in a large serving bowl.

Per serving (1 scant cup): 346 Cal, 5 g Fat, 1 g Sat Fat, 0 mg Chol, 699 mg Sod, 64 g Carb, 4 g Fib, 11 g Prot, 43 mg Calc. *POINTS: 7.*

FIVE-STAR TIP   Some, thin Japanese wheat-flour noodles, can be purchased in many supermarkets or in Asian groceries. You can also use linguine or lo mein noodles.

Thai-Style Peanut Noodles
and Thai Egg Drop Soup

QUICK LIST

fresh corn
garlic oil
shrimp
jalapeño pepper
radiatore

Pasta with Pan-Roasted Corn and Shrimp

MAKES 4 SERVINGS

If you haven't tried radiatore yet, this recipe is a good excuse to do so. Italian for "radiators," this chunky ruffled-shaped pasta is ideal paired with lighter sauces, because every drop will cling to its ridges. We prefer using fresh corn for this dish because of its superior taste and texture when pan-roasted. But that's no problem during the winter months any longer—thanks to supersweet fresh corn from the South, now widely available in the produce aisle.

3 ears of corn, kernels removed (about 2 cups)
1 tablespoon garlic oil
1 pound large shrimp, peeled and deveined
1 jalapeño pepper, seeded and minced (wear gloves to prevent irritation)
½ pound radiatore
½ teaspoon salt

1. Heat a 12-inch nonstick skillet over medium-high heat. Add the corn and cook until lightly charred in spots, 2 minutes. Transfer to a large serving bowl.
2. Return the same pan to the heat. Add the garlic oil, then add the shrimp and jalapeño in a single layer. Cook the shrimp until browned, 1–1½ minutes on each side. Add the shrimp mixture to the corn.
3. Meanwhile, cook the radiatore according to package directions. Drain, reserving ½ cup of the cooking liquid. Add the radiatore, the reserved liquid, and the salt to the shrimp and corn mixture; toss to coat.

Per serving (about 1 cup): 370 Cal, 6 g Fat, 1 g Sat Fat, 135 mg Chol, 460 mg Sod, 57 g Carb, 4 g Fib, 25 g Prot, 40 mg Calc. **POINTS: 7.**

turkey pepperoni
canned diced tomatoes
littleneck clams
linguine
parsley

QUICK LIST

Linguine with Clams and Pepperoni

MAKES 4 SERVINGS

Tasty turkey pepperoni and diced tomatoes with jalapeño peppers make this streamlined version of classic red clam sauce a winner. We suggest linguine *fine* (a thinner style of linguine) for the dish, but you can also use vermicelli or spaghettini, if desired.

½ cup thinly sliced, ready-to-eat turkey pepperoni (1½ ounces)

1 (14½-ounce) can diced tomatoes with jalapeños

½ cup water

2 dozen littleneck clams, scrubbed

½ pound linguine fine

¼ cup chopped parsley

1. Spray a large saucepan with nonstick spray and set over medium-high heat. Add the pepperoni and cook until just golden, 2–3 minutes. Add the tomatoes and water; reduce the heat and simmer 5 minutes.

2. Add the clams, cover, increase the heat, and bring to a boil. Cook until the clams open, 5–7 minutes. Discard any clams that have not opened.

3. Meanwhile, cook the linguine according to package directions. Drain and toss with the clam mixture and parsley in a large warm serving bowl. Serve at once.

Per serving (about 1 cup linguine with 6 clams): 434 Cal, 5 g Fat, 1 g Sat Fat, 88 mg Chol, 947 mg Sod, 55 g Carb, 3 g Fib, 40 g Prot, 158 mg Calc. ***POINTS: 8.***

FIVE-STAR TIP   To quickly warm the serving bowl, pour the hot cooking liquid into the bowl when draining the pasta; let stand one to two minutes. Carefully tip the bowl to pour out the hot water, then quickly dry the bowl with a clean kitchen towel.

QUICK LIST

bacon
sea scallops
onion
clam juice
mini penne

Pasta with Scallops and Bacon

MAKES 6 SERVINGS

If used wisely, bacon can play an important role in healthy cooking, because it's terrific at boosting the flavor of whatever it's paired with and very little goes a long way. Bacon's smoky, salty taste marries particularly well with sweet, succulent scallops, so we sear the scallops in a skillet with bacon drippings over very high heat. Seared properly, the scallops should be deep golden on the outside, translucent and very tender inside, so don't be tempted to overcook them.

2 slices bacon
1 pound sea scallops
½ teaspoon salt
¼ teaspoon freshly
  ground pepper
1 medium onion, diced
1 (8-ounce) bottle or
  1 (10-ounce) can
  clam juice
½ pound mini penne

1. To prepare the sauce, cook the bacon in a large nonstick skillet until crisp-cooked. Transfer to a cutting board with tongs and finely chop, reserving the drippings in the skillet. Set the chopped bacon aside.

2. Pat the scallops dry with paper towels; sprinkle with the salt and pepper. Heat the drippings in the same skillet over high heat. Add half the scallops and cook until deep golden, 2 minutes on each side. Transfer to a plate and repeat.

3. Reduce the heat; add the onion and cook until deep golden, 5–6 minutes. Add the clam juice and bring to a boil; reduce the heat and cook at a low boil until slightly reduced, 2–3 minutes. Add the scallops and stir until just heated through, 1 minute.

4. Meanwhile, cook the mini penne according to package directions. Drain and toss with the sauce in a large serving bowl. Sprinkle with the reserved bacon and serve.

Per serving (1 cup): 205 Cal, 5 g Fat, 1 g Sat Fat, 18 mg Chol, 543 mg Sod, 27 g Carb, 1 g Fib, 12 g Prot, 19 mg Calc. **POINTS: 4.**

FIVE-STAR TIP If you're feeling generous with ingredients, any fresh herb will add sparkle to this dish—parsley, cilantro, basil, oregano, or tarragon are just some of the tasty options. Sprinkle 2 tablespoons finely chopped herbs of your choice over the pasta just before serving.

QUICK LIST

small shells
red onion
light mayonnaise
lemon juice
canned tuna

Tuna Pasta Salad

MAKES 4 SERVINGS

If you're a fan of macaroni salad, you're going to love this interpretation with delicate small shell pasta, lemony mayo dressing, and tuna. Rinsing the chopped red onion under cold water helps reduce its sharp taste. If you want the dressing to have a thinner consistency, add the optional one tablespoon of water.

1 cup small shells

⅓ cup finely chopped red onion

3 tablespoons light mayonnaise

1 tablespoon fresh lemon juice

½ teaspoon salt

¼ teaspoon freshly ground pepper

1 (6-ounce) can water-packed tuna, drained and flaked

1 tablespoon water (optional)

1. Cook the shells according to package directions. Drain and rinse with cold water. Add the onions to the shells and rinse again.

2. Combine the mayonnaise, lemon juice, salt, and pepper in a large serving bowl; stir in the tuna. Add the shells mixture and the water, if using, and toss.

Per serving (¾ cup): 175 Cal, 5 g Fat, 1 g Sat Fat, 19 mg Chol, 516 mg Sod, 20 g Carb, 1 g Fib, 12 g Prot, 13 mg Calc. **POINTS: 4.**

FIVE-STAR TIP The salad can be refrigerated in an airtight container for up to a day. Let stand at room temperature 15 minutes before serving, adding another tablespoon of water, if necessary.

Moroccan-Style Ziti with Chicken

MAKES 4 SERVINGS

Diced tomatoes seasoned with garlic and basil, as well as a touch of curry powder, add exotic flair to this tasty pasta entrée. Normally, this chicken mixture would be served over couscous, but we think ziti makes a much heartier pairing.

1 pound skinless boneless chicken thighs, trimmed of all visible fat and cut into 1-inch pieces

½ teaspoon salt

¼ teaspoon freshly ground pepper

1 medium onion, diced

½ teaspoon curry powder

1 (14½-ounce) can diced tomatoes with Italian herbs

½ pound ziti or penne

1. To prepare the sauce, sprinkle the chicken with the salt and pepper. Heat a 12-inch nonstick skillet and set over high heat. Add the chicken and cook, turning the pieces as they brown, 4 minutes. Transfer the chicken to a plate and set aside.

2. Reduce the heat, add the onion, and cook until lightly browned, 4 minutes. Stir in the curry powder and cook until fragrant, 1 minute. Return the chicken to the skillet, add the tomatoes, and bring to a boil. Reduce the heat, cover, and simmer until the flavors blend and the chicken is cooked through, 20 minutes.

3. Meanwhile, cook the ziti according to package directions. Drain and toss with the sauce in a large serving bowl.

Per serving (1¾ cups): 399 Cal, 9 g Fat, 2 g Sat Fat, 77 mg Chol, 887 mg Sod, 48 g Carb, 3 g Fib, 29 g Prot, 90 mg Calc. ***POINTS: 8.***

large shrimp
curry powder
chicken thighs
fresh ginger
capellini

QUICK LIST

Singapore Noodles

MAKES 4 SERVINGS

Traditionally prepared with bits of chopped shrimp, diced chicken, curry powder, and fried rice noodles, this zesty dish is served in roadside noodle shops throughout Singapore. To keep the noodles on the healthy side, we use capellini instead of the rice noodles and skip the frying, then add freshly grated ginger to the sauce, which boosts its spicy taste.

¾ pound large shrimp, peeled and deveined

3 teaspoons curry powder

½ pound skinless boneless chicken thighs, trimmed of all visible fat and diced

3 teaspoons grated peeled fresh ginger

¾ teaspoon salt

½ pound capellini

1. Toss the shrimp with 2 teaspoons of the curry powder. Toss the chicken with 2 teaspoons of the ginger and ½ teaspoon of the salt.

2. Heat a 12-inch nonstick skillet over high heat. Add the chicken and cook until browned, 2–2½ minutes on each side. Transfer the chicken to a large bowl.

3. Add the shrimp to the same skillet; cook until golden brown, 1½ minutes on each side. Transfer the shrimp to a cutting board and coarsely chop.

4. Cook the capellini according to package directions. Drain, reserving 1½ cups of the cooking liquid. Rinse the capellini briefly with warm water (to help keep strands separated).

5. Meanwhile, prepare the sauce: Set the same skillet over medium heat. Add the remaining 1 teaspoon curry powder and 1 teaspoon ginger. Heat the spices, stirring, until just fragrant, 15–25 seconds. Carefully stir in the reserved liquid and simmer until blended, 10–20 seconds. Add the reserved chicken, the shrimp, and the remaining ¼ teaspoon salt; simmer until the sauce is just heated through, 1 minute. Toss the capellini and the sauce in a large serving bowl. Serve at once.

Per serving (1½ cups): 302 Cal, 6 g Fat, 1 g Sat Fat, 139 mg Chol, 777 mg Sod, 33 g Carb, 2 g Fib, 29 g Prot, 33 mg Calc. **POINTS: 6.**

QUICK LIST

brown lentils
onion
smoked ham
chicken broth
campanile

Smoky Ham and Lentil Pasta

MAKES 6 SERVINGS

Pasta and lentils are a classic Italian combination. In this version, just a little bit of smoked ham (versus a whole lot of oil) goes a long way in adding flavor. Look for premium-quality smoked ham in the deli section of the supermarket.

1 cup brown lentils, sorted and rinsed

1 medium onion, cut into thin wedges

4 ounces lean smoked ham (5% or less fat), diced

1¼ cups low-sodium chicken broth

8 ounces campanile (bell-shaped pasta)

1. Bring 4 cups water to a boil in a medium saucepan. Add the lentils and cook until they are tender but still hold their shape, 12–16 minutes. Drain and rinse with cold water until cool. Set aside.

2. Spray a large nonstick skillet with nonstick spray and set over medium-low heat. Add the onion and cook until well-browned and tender, 15 minutes. Increase the heat; add the ham and cook until lightly browned, 2 minutes. Add the broth, bring to a boil, and boil 1 minute.

3. Meanwhile, cook the campanile according to package directions. Drain and toss with the onion-broth mixture and the lentils in a large serving bowl.

Per serving (about 1 cup): 267 Cal, 2 g Fat, 1 g Sat Fat, 10 mg Chol, 191 mg Sod, 47 g Carb, 8 g Fib, 17 g Prot, 30 mg Calc. *POINTS: 5.*

FIVE-STAR TIP You can also serve this pasta at room temperature. Prepare the recipe as directed, except cool the onion-broth mixture until lukewarm and rinse the cooked pasta with cool water until warm. The dish can stand, covered, at room temperature up to an hour.

ground veal
garlic
chicken broth
oregano
mezze rigatoni

QUICK LIST

Pasta with Mediterranean Veal Sauce

MAKES 4 SERVINGS

Mezze means "half" in Italian, and many of the new pasta shapes are pint-size versions of the classics, like the mezze rigatoni in this recipe. And, just like regular rigatoni, its robust shape pairs well with meat sauces. Fresh oregano is an essential part of this dish, because its pungent flavor beautifully complements the milder-tasting ingredients. If you would prefer not to use veal, substitute an equal amount of ground skinless chicken (the **POINTS** per serving will remain the same).

¾ **pound lean ground veal (10% or less fat)**

3 **large cloves garlic, crushed through a press**

1¼ **cups low-sodium chicken broth**

1½ **teaspoons minced oregano**

¾ **teaspoon salt**

¼ **teaspoon freshly ground pepper**

½ **pound mezze rigatoni**

1. To prepare the sauce, spray a 12-inch nonstick skillet with nonstick spray and set over medium-high heat. Add the veal and brown, breaking it apart with a spoon, 10–12 minutes. Stir in the garlic and cook until fragrant, 1 minute. Add the broth, oregano, salt, and pepper; reduce the heat and simmer 2 minutes.

2. Meanwhile, cook the mezze rigatoni according to package directions. Drain and toss with the sauce in a large serving bowl.

Per serving (1¾ cups): 303 Cal, 6 g Fat, 2 g Sat Fat, 53 mg Chol, 515 mg Sod, 43 g Carb, 2 g Fib, 21 g Prot, 32 mg Calc. **POINTS: 6.**

FIVE-STAR TIP The sauce may be cooled, then refrigerated in an airtight container for up to three days. To reheat, transfer the sauce to a 3-quart saucepan and cook, stirring occasionally, over medium heat about 15 minutes.

**Rigatoni with Hearty
Pork-and-Tomato Sauce**

Rigatoni with Hearty Pork-and-Tomato Sauce

QUICK LIST

canned whole tomatoes
boneless pork chops
garlic
fennel seeds
rigatoni

MAKES 8 SERVINGS

A perfect choice for a Sunday-night supper with friends, this robust tomato sauce, with braised pork and fennel, actually improves if prepared ahead. There's virtually no fussy prep required for the sauce, just a long, slow simmer to bring out the luscious melding of meat and tomato flavors. For best results, use a heavy-bottomed Dutch oven with a tight-fitting lid to cook the sauce.

1 (28-ounce) can whole tomatoes in juice
1 (14–16-ounce) can whole tomatoes in juice
2 pounds boneless pork loin chops (¾–1-inch thick), trimmed of all visible fat
4 large cloves garlic, finely chopped
½ teaspoon fennel seeds, crushed
1 teaspoon salt
½ teaspoon freshly ground pepper
1 pound rigatoni

1. Preheat the oven to 325°F.

2. Puree the 2 cans of tomatoes with their juice in batches in a blender; set aside.

3. Spray a large Dutch oven with nonstick cooking spray and set over medium-high heat. Add the pork and cook until browned, 2 minutes on each side. Transfer to a plate and set aside.

4. Add the garlic and fennel to the same Dutch oven. Reduce the heat and cook until the garlic is just fragrant and beginning to color, about 1 minute. Add the pureed tomatoes and bring to a boil. Add the pork, cover, and transfer the pot to the oven. Bake until the pork is just tender, 1½ hours. Stir in the salt and pepper. Bake, uncovered, until the pork is fork-tender and the sauce is slightly thickened, 30 minutes more.

5. Transfer the pork with tongs to a cutting board. When cool enough to handle, dice. Stir pork back into the sauce.

6. Meanwhile, cook the rigatoni according to package directions. Drain and toss with half the sauce in a large serving bowl; pour the remaining sauce over the top.

Per serving (1½ cups pasta with generous ¾ cup sauce): 410 Cal, 9 g Fat, 3 g Sat Fat, 68 mg Chol, 557 mg Sod, 48 g Carb, 4 g Fib, 34 g Prot, 77 mg Calc. *POINTS: 8.*

Chapter 4

fast food

30-minute (or less) main courses

QUICK LIST

bean thread noodles
chicken broth
star anise
tofu
bok choy

Chinese Four-Treasure Soup

MAKES 6 SERVINGS

Yes, there are five ingredients, but just four treasures (in classic Cantonese cooking, you don't count the broth). This simple soup is a variation of the traditional "purification" soup, served the day after a New Year's banquet in some Chinese homes. Bean threads, or cellophane noodles, are made from the starch of green mung beans. They can be found in the ethnic section of many supermarkets and in Asian groceries.

2 ounces bean threads (cellophane noodles)

4 cups hot water

2 (14½-ounce) cans fat-free, low-sodium chicken broth

3 star anise pods

1 (12¾-ounce) package extra-firm low-fat tofu, cut into ½-inch pieces

½ pound bok choy, coarsely chopped (about 4 cups)

½ teaspoon freshly ground pepper

1. Place the noodles in a large bowl and add enough hot water to cover; let stand until the noodles are soft, 10 minutes. Drain and cut into 3-inch strands.

2. Meanwhile, combine the chicken broth and star anise in a large pot and bring to a boil. Reduce the heat and simmer, covered, until flavors are blended, 15 minutes.

3. Remove the star anise with a slotted spoon and discard. Stir in the tofu and bok choy. Simmer, covered, until the bok choy is tender, about 5 minutes. Add the noodles and pepper. Simmer until heated through, 2 minutes.

Per serving (1 cup): 67 Cal, 1 g Fat, 0 g Sat Fat, 0 mg Chol, 449 mg Sod, 10 g Carb, 0 g Fib, 5 g Prot, 66 mg Calc. **POINTS: 1.**

FIVE-STAR TIP This soup can be stored, covered, in the refrigerator up to a day. Reheat in a microwave on High for 5 minutes, stirring once. If you would prefer to skip the tofu, prepare the recipe as directed and add ½ pound shredded cooked chicken breast instead of the tofu in Step 3 (for **2 POINTS** per serving).

Speedy Vegetable Gumbo

canned red kidney beans
canned diced tomatoes
frozen cut okra
green bell pepper
seasoned rice mix

QUICK LIST

MAKES 6 SERVINGS

Gumbo is a Creole dish, a staple among the Louisiana people descended from African slaves, French traders, and Native Americans. Gumbo, in fact, means "okra" in several West African dialects—and okra, thanks to its gelatinous properties, actually thickens the dish. Gumbo usually involves multiple tasks and a lengthy cooking time. But thanks to the convenience of canned beans, seasoned tomatoes, and rice mix, this version is practically foolproof and on the table in a flash.

1 (15-ounce) can red kidney beans or black beans, rinsed and drained

1 (14½-ounce) can fat-free diced tomatoes with green chiles

1 (10-ounce) package frozen cut okra, thawed

1 green bell pepper, seeded and chopped

2 cups water

1 (7½-ounce) package low-sodium seasoned rice mix (e.g., Casbah Spanish Pilaf or Casbah Nutted Pilaf)

Combine the beans, tomatoes, okra, bell pepper, and water in a large saucepan and bring to a boil. Reduce the heat and simmer, covered, 5 minutes. Stir in the rice mix and simmer, covered, until the rice is tender, about 20 minutes.

Per serving (1 generous cup): 121 Cal, 1 g Fat, 0 g Sat Fat, 0 mg Chol, 329 mg Sod, 23 g Carb, 5 g Fib, 5 g Prot, 114 mg Calc. **POINTS: 2.**

No-Fuss Cioppino

marinara sauce
dry vermouth
frozen mixed vegetables
shrimp
cod fillets

QUICK LIST

No-Fuss Cioppino

MAKES 6 SERVINGS

It might sound like it comes from Naples, but cioppino is an American dish through and through. It was first developed in San Francisco by Italian immigrants trying to re-create the taste of their homeland with the bounty of American ingredients. Usually, it's a heady stew that takes hours, but with store-bought marinara sauce and frozen mixed vegetables, it's ready in a snap. Serve with crusty bread and a tossed green salad.

1 (26-ounce) jar fat-free
   marinara sauce

½ cup dry vermouth

1 (16-ounce) package
   frozen mixed vegetables,
   thawed

½ pound medium shrimp,
   peeled and deveined

1 pound boneless cod
   fillets, cut into
   1-inch cubes

1 teaspoon freshly
   ground pepper

Combine the marinara sauce and vermouth in a large pot and bring to a boil. Add the mixed vegetables, shrimp, and cod. Reduce the heat and simmer, covered, until the cod and shrimp are opaque in the center, about 10 minutes. Stir in the pepper.

Per serving (about 1½ cups): 166 Cal, 2 g Fat, 0 g Sat Fat, 74 mg Chol, 487 mg Sod, 21 g Carb, 5 g Fib, 18 g Prot, 114 mg Calc. *POINTS: 3.*

FIVE-STAR TIP The delicate, mild flavor of cod fillet works well in this dish, but you can also use flounder, snapper, or halibut fillets with equally delicious results. There are a wide variety of frozen mixed vegetables available—broccoli, corn, and red peppers or broccoli, red pepper, onion, and mushrooms are two blends that would work well in this hearty entrée.

QUICK LIST

tomato soup

saffron

littleneck clams

frozen peas

couscous

Couscous "Paella"

MAKES 8 SERVINGS

Technically, paella isn't food—it's the pan the dish is cooked in. But we've overlooked the technicality, and tradition, in this unorthodox recipe. We replace the rice with saffron-scented couscous (so no paella pan is required) and add quick-cooking clams so you get all the flavor of this Spanish favorite without the wait.

1 (15-ounce) can fat-free, low-sodium tomato soup or tomato soup with roasted garlic

1 cup water

⅛ teaspoon saffron

36 littleneck clams (about 1¾ pounds), scrubbed

1 (10-ounce) package frozen peas, thawed

1 (10-ounce) box plain couscous

1. Combine the tomato soup, water, and saffron in a large pot and bring to a boil. Add the clams, cover, reduce the heat, and simmer until they open, about 6 minutes. Discard any clams that have not opened.

2. Stir in the peas, then the couscous. Cover and remove from the heat; let stand 5 minutes. Fluff the couscous and the rest of the ingredients with a fork.

Per serving (about 1 cup): 303 Cal, 2 g Fat, 0 g Sat Fat, 56 mg Chol, 191 mg Sod, 40 g Carb, 5 g Fib, 29 g Prot, 103 mg Calc. **POINTS: 5.**

FIVE-STAR TIP Because saffron is a rare, expensive spice, it's sometimes only available at the manager's desk in supermarkets. This recipe works well with any variety of small clams, such as pismos or butter clams.

onion
hominy
canned tomatoes
chicken breasts
tomatillo sauce

QUICK LIST

Quick Posole

MAKES 6 SERVINGS

Posole is a thick, hearty Mexican stew with hominy (white or yellow corn kernels with the hull and germ removed). Our version includes the traditional ingredients: chicken, tomatoes, and onions—as well as the untraditional tomatillo sauce. Often garnished with shredded cheese, sliced radishes, chopped cilantro, and lettuce, posole makes a colorful and festive party dish.

1 medium onion, finely chopped

1 (30-ounce) can hominy, rinsed and drained

1 (28-ounce) can tomatoes (no salt added), drained and chopped

1 pound skinless boneless chicken breasts, cut into ½-inch pieces

1½ cups water

¾ cup tomatillo sauce or salsa verde

½ teaspoon freshly ground pepper

1. Spray a large nonstick pot with nonstick spray and set over medium heat. Add the onion and cook until softened, about 3 minutes.

2. Add the hominy, tomatoes, chicken, water, and tomatillo sauce; bring to a boil. Reduce the heat and simmer, covered, stirring often, 15 minutes. Add the pepper. Simmer, uncovered, until slightly thickened, about 5 minutes longer.

Per serving (generous 1 cup): 190 Cal, 3 g Fat, 1 g Sat Fat, 42 mg Chol, 264 mg Sod, 23 g Carb, 4 g Fib, 18 g Prot, 60 mg Calc. *POINTS: 3.*

FIVE-STAR TIP   Tomatillo sauce and salsa verde are both available mild, medium, or hot, so select according to your taste.

QUICK LIST

basmati rice
mango chutney
chicken breasts
dried cranberries
pecan halves

Tropical Basmati Rice Salad

MAKES 6 SERVINGS

In Hindi, basmati translates as "queen of fragrance," and this rice, grown for centuries on the slopes of the Himalayas, is indeed that: nutty, woody, and very aromatic. It used to be quite expensive, but thanks to farms in Texas, it's now readily available in American markets—making a great base for this main-course salad. Buy the cooked chicken at the deli counter; or buy a whole roasted chicken, slice off the breast meat you need, and reserve the rest for another use, like your child's lunch or an easy chicken salad.

1 cup basmati, Texmati, or long-grain white rice
1¾ cups + 2 tablespoons water
¾ cup mango chutney
12 ounces chopped cooked chicken breast
½ cup dried cranberries
½ cup pecan halves, toasted and chopped
¾ teaspoon freshly ground pepper

1. Combine the rice and 1¾ cups of the water in a medium saucepan and bring to a boil. Reduce the heat and simmer, covered, until the rice is tender and the water is absorbed, about 20 minutes. Fluff the rice with a fork.

2. Meanwhile, combine the chutney and the remaining 2 tablespoons of the water in a small saucepan. Cook over low heat, stirring constantly, until chutney melts and the mixture is smooth, about 1 minute.

3. Combine the rice, chicken, cranberries, pecans, and pepper in a large bowl. Toss with the melted chutney.

Per serving (1 cup): 361 Cal, 9 g Fat, 1 g Sat Fat, 48 mg Chol, 340 mg Sod, 53 g Carb, 3 g Fib, 21 g Prot, 27 mg Calc. ***POINTS: 7.***

FIVE-STAR TIP This dish is great for leftovers; just store in an airtight container and refrigerate up to two days. You can also make this salad using cooked wild rice. Since wild rice can take up to an hour to make, it's much quicker in the pressure cooker. Just cook 1 cup wild rice and 3 cups water according to the manufacturer's directions, 23 to 27 minutes.

Pita Pizzas

MAKES 6 SERVINGS

If you love a thin, crisp pizza crust, this healthy pie is for you. Pita bread makes a nifty pizza base that's ideal for a variety of speedy toppings. Look for fat-free pitas in gourmet markets and specialty bakeries.

6 ounces cremini mushrooms, sliced (2½ cups)

6 (5-inch) fat-free pitas

¾ cup fat-free pizza sauce

¼ cup sliced pitted black olives

1½ cups shredded fat-free mozzarella cheese

½ teaspoon freshly ground pepper

1. Preheat the oven to 450°F. Spray a large nonstick skillet with nonstick spray and set over medium heat. Add the mushrooms and cook until softened and the excess moisture has evaporated, about 5 minutes.

2. Place the pitas on a large baking sheet. Top each with 2 tablespoons of the pizza sauce, 2 tablespoons of the mushrooms, 2 teaspoons of the olives, and ¼ cup of the mozzarella. Sprinkle a pinch of pepper over each.

3. Bake the pizzas until hot and the cheese lightly browns, about 12 minutes. Transfer to a rack and cool 5 minutes before serving.

Per serving (1 pizza): 185 Cal, 1 g Fat, 0 g Sat Fat, 3 mg Chol, 546 mg Sod, 28 g Carb, 2 g Fib, 15 g Prot, 257 mg Calc. **POINTS: 3.**

FIVE-STAR TIP These completely cooked pizzas can be wrapped tightly in plastic wrap and refrigerated overnight. When ready to eat, reheat in a 350°F oven for 10 minutes.

Instant Polenta with
Sautéed Vegetables

Instant Polenta with Sautéed Vegetables

shiitake mushrooms
frozen peas
dry vermouth
instant polenta
Parmesan cheese

QUICK LIST

MAKES 4 SERVINGS

Preparing polenta used to be a labor-intensive and time-consuming task—but no more! Thanks to instant (or quick-cooking) packaged polenta, it takes a mere five minutes to get this creamy Italian favorite on the table. We've paired it with a simple vegetable sauté, which makes this cheesy soft polenta a one-dish meal.

8 large shiitake mushrooms (6 ounces), stemmed and thinly sliced

1 (10-ounce) package frozen peas, thawed

½ cup dry vermouth

½ teaspoon freshly ground pepper

¼ teaspoon + ½ teaspoon salt

4 cups water

1 cup instant polenta

3 tablespoons grated Parmesan cheese

1. Spray a large skillet with nonstick spray and set over medium-high heat. Add the mushrooms and cook until softened, about 2 minutes. Add the peas and cook 1 minute. Add the vermouth, bring to a boil, and cook until it reduces slightly, about 1 minute. Stir in the pepper and ¼ teaspoon of the salt. Set aside and keep warm.

2. Meanwhile, prepare the polenta: Combine the water and the remaining ½ teaspoon of the salt in a medium saucepan and bring to a boil. Stirring constantly, gradually add the polenta in a slow, steady stream; reduce the heat and cook, stirring, until thick but not stiff, 5 minutes. Remove from the heat and stir in the Parmesan.

3. Divide the polenta on each of 4 serving plates and top with the vegetable mixture. Serve at once.

Per serving (1 cup polenta with ½ cup vegetable mixture): 277 Cal, 2 g Fat, 1 g Sat Fat, 4 mg Chol, 605 mg Sod, 51 g Carb, 7 g Fib, 13 g Prot, 83 mg Calc. **POINTS: 5.**

FIVE-STAR TIP If dry vermouth isn't handy, you can substitute dry white wine.

QUICK LIST

mangoes
fresh pineapple
whole wheat tortillas
farmer cheese
canned enchilada sauce

New World Enchiladas

MAKES 6 SERVINGS

These enchiladas are hardly traditional: a little bit of the Caribbean (the mango), a touch of the South Pacific (the pineapple), and a dab of the United States (the cheese), all bound together in a healthy whole-wheat tortilla. Use two wide spatulas to remove each delicate yet generously filled baked enchilada from the pan.

2 ripe mangoes, peeled, pitted, and coarsely chopped

½ pound fresh pineapple, coarsely chopped (1½ cups)

6 (8-inch) whole-wheat tortillas

6 ounces crumbled farmer cheese or fat-free ricotta (¾ cup)

1 (15-ounce) can enchilada sauce

1. Preheat the oven to 400°F. Spray a 9 × 13-inch baking dish with nonstick spray and set aside.
2. Combine the mangoes and pineapple in a medium bowl.
3. Place one tortilla on a work surface. Place ½ cup fruit mixture in the center, then top with 2 tablespoons of the cheese. Roll up and place seam-side-down in the baking pan. Repeat with the remaining tortillas, fruit mixture, and cheese. Spoon the enchilada sauce over the top. Bake until the sauce is bubbly and the cheese begins to melt, 20 minutes. Let stand 5 minutes before serving.

Per serving (1 enchilada): 273 Cal, 11 g Fat, 6 g Sat Fat, 25 mg Chol, 590 mg Sod, 42 g Carb, 4 g Fib, 10 g Prot, 222 mg Calc. **POINTS: 6.**

FIVE-STAR TIP   Farmer cheese is a drier version of cottage cheese (most of the liquid has been pressed out). Some varieties are dry and crumbly, while others are firm enough to be sliced. It has a mild, slightly tangy flavor.

QUICK LIST

red potatoes
green beans
tuna steak
Boston lettuce
dill dressing

Easy Salad Niçoise

MAKES 4 SERVINGS

Salad Niçoise, long popular on the French Riviera, is a composed salad—meaning it's a salad that isn't tossed but arranged on the plate, then dressed. It's traditionally served with seared tuna, so buy only the freshest you can find. To check for freshness, always ask to smell the tuna: It should have a clean and bright fragrance, like the breeze off the ocean.

12 small red potatoes (about 10 ounces)

6 cups water

2½ cups green beans (about 8 ounces), trimmed

1 pound tuna steak (about ¾-inch thick)

1 head Boston lettuce, torn

½ cup fat-free creamy dill dressing

1. Combine the potatoes and water in a large pot; bring to a boil over medium-high heat. Cook, covered, 7 minutes. Add the green beans and cook, uncovered, until the potatoes are tender and the beans are tender-crisp, 3 minutes. Drain and rinse with cool water until cool.

2. Spray a large skillet with nonstick spray and set over high heat. Cook the tuna until just pink in the center, 5–6 minutes on each side. Transfer the tuna to a cutting board and thinly slice.

3. Place 1½ cups of the lettuce, 3 potatoes, one-fourth of the green beans, and one-fourth of the tuna on each of 4 serving plates. Top each serving with the dressing.

Per serving (about 3 cups with 2 tablespoons dressing): 206 Cal, 1 g Fat, 0 g Sat Fat, 49 mg Chol, 366 mg Sod, 17 g Carb, 3 g Fib, 30 g Prot, 76 mg Calc. **POINTS: 4.**

FIVE-STAR TIP If you like it rare, you can cook the tuna only 3 minutes on each side. For a super-simple supper, use canned tuna.

QUICK LIST

jumbo lump crabmeat
fat-free mayonnaise
sweet pickle relish
scallions
hot dog buns

Maine Crab Rolls

MAKES 4 SERVINGS

The minute you enter the state of Maine, lobster- and crab-roll shacks start popping up at highway exits and along side roads. No wonder—these Down-East favorites make for speedy summer lunches or dinners, especially when made with purchased lump crabmeat. For an authentic taste, toast the hot dog buns cut-side down on the grill or toaster-oven rack.

12 ounces cooked jumbo
    lump crabmeat,
    picked over
¼ cup fat-free mayonnaise
2 tablespoons sweet
    pickle relish
2 scallions, thinly sliced
½ teaspoon freshly
    ground pepper
4 hot dog buns

1. In a large bowl, gently combine the crabmeat, mayonnaise, pickle relish, scallions, and pepper.
2. Split each bun and fill with the crab mixture.

Per serving (1 roll with generous ½ cup filling): 239 Cal, 5 g Fat, 1 g Sat Fat, 87 mg Chol, 935 mg Sod, 27 g Carb, 2 g Fib, 21 g Prot, 146 mg Calc. ***POINTS: 5.***

FIVE-STAR TIP Lump crabmeat is delicious, but it also can be expensive. Use shredded imitation crabmeat or drained canned crabmeat, if desired.

Maine Crab Rolls

QUICK LIST

soy sauce
lemon juice
honey
tuna fillet
panko

Fusion-Style Tuna Cakes

MAKES 4 SERVINGS

East meets West in these fabulous fish cakes, seasoned with soy sauce, lemon juice, and honey, then coated with panko, coarse-and-dry Japanese bread crumbs. (Panko is commonly sold in Asian groceries.) Pulse the tuna in the food processor only until it looks like ground turkey, so the texture of the cakes will have some bite when cooked.

2 tablespoons reduced-sodium soy sauce

2 tablespoons fresh lemon juice

2 tablespoons honey

1 pound tuna fillet, cut into 2-inch cubes

⅔ cup panko (Japanese dry bread crumbs) or dry bread crumbs

1. Combine the soy sauce, lemon juice, and honey until smooth in a small bowl. Set aside.

2. Pulse the tuna in a food processor until coarsely chopped. Transfer to a large bowl and stir in ¼ cup of the bread crumbs and half of the soy sauce mixture. Form into 4 cakes. Set aside the remaining soy sauce mixture for the sauce.

3. Place the remaining bread crumbs onto a plate; add the cakes, gently pressing the crumbs into the cakes, turning to coat evenly.

4. Spray a large nonstick skillet with nonstick spray and set over medium heat. Add the tuna cakes and cook until brown, 3½ minutes on each side.

5. Transfer the cakes to a large plate and keep warm. Add the reserved soy sauce mixture to the same skillet and boil over high heat, scraping up the browned bits from the bottom of the pan, until reduced to a thin glaze, 5 seconds. Divide the sauce among 4 plates; top each serving with a tuna cake.

Per serving (1 tuna cake with 1 teaspoon sauce): 184 Cal, 1 g Fat, 0 g Sat Fat, 49 mg Chol, 357 mg Sod, 15 g Carb, 0 g Fib, 27 g Prot, 20 mg Calc. *POINTS: 4.*

fat-free yogurt
curry powder
pork tenderloin
onion
lemon juice

QUICK LIST

Pork Tandoori

MAKES 4 SERVINGS

Tandoori is a popular dish in Indian restaurants. In traditional tandoori, the meat is marinated in yogurt and a blend of spices, often a chef's carefully guarded secret. Here, curry powder eliminates the need for multiple ingredients and simplifies the process. Let the pork marinate at room temperature 10 minutes, but no longer, since the yogurt breaks down the meat and will make it chewy. If you want a hotter dish, try Madras curry powder, a spice blend made with more cayenne.

1 cup plain fat-free yogurt

1 tablespoon curry powder

1 (1-pound) pork tenderloin, trimmed of all visible fat

1 large onion, cut into eighths

Juice of 1 lemon

1. To prepare the marinade, combine the yogurt and curry powder in a small bowl. Place the pork in a shallow dish; pour the marinade on top and turn the pork to coat. Let stand at room temperature, 10 minutes.

2. Meanwhile, spray the broiler rack with nonstick spray; preheat the broiler.

3. Scrape the excess marinade from the pork and discard. Broil the pork 5 inches from the heat, 8 minutes. Turn the pork, add the onions to the pan, and broil, turning the onions once if they become too brown, until the internal temperature of the pork reaches 160°F, 8 minutes longer.

4. To serve, squeeze the lemon juice over the pork and onions. Transfer the pork to a cutting board and slice. Serve with the onions.

Per serving (¼ of pork with ¼ cup onions): 160 Cal, 4 g Fat, 1 g Sat Fat, 68 mg Chol, 57 mg Sod, 5 g Carb, 1 g Fib, 25 g Prot, 32 mg Calc.
POINTS: 3.

FIVE-STAR TIP This dish also works beautifully with 1 pound skinless boneless chicken breasts for the same amount of **POINTS** per serving. (Marinate this version in the refrigerator one hour or overnight.) To save on cleanup, line a baking pan with foil and spray the foil with nonstick spray. When you're done, simply throw away the foil.

chicken sausage
fresh corn
green bell peppers
pineapple
creamy garlic dressing

Zesty Sausage, Vegetable, and Pineapple Kebabs

MAKES 4 SERVINGS

These speedy broiled skewers are sure to become an instant family favorite. A slathering of garlicky fat-free salad dressing is the secret to their big, bold taste. Slash the prep time by using fresh-cut pineapple and ready-to-eat fresh corn on the cob from your supermarket's produce section.

12 ounces fresh chicken sausage, (e.g., Bilinki's Chicken Sausage with Sundried Tomato and Basil or Hans' All Natural Chicken Sausage with Green Onions), cut into 8 (2-inch) pieces

2 ears of corn

1 large green bell pepper, seeded and cut into 8 chunks

8 (1-inch) pineapple chunks

4 tablespoons fat-free creamy garlic dressing

1. Fill a large saucepan two-thirds full of water and bring to a boil. Add the sausage, reduce the heat, and simmer until cooked through, 10 minutes. Drain the sausage and cool 5 minutes.

2. Meanwhile, line the broiler pan with foil and spray with nonstick spray; preheat the broiler. Husk the corn and remove any corn silk; cut each ear crosswise into 4 pieces.

3. Alternately thread 2 pieces of the sausage, corn, bell pepper, and pineapple onto each of 4 (12-inch) metal skewers. Brush each kebab with 1 tablespoon dressing.

4. Place the kebabs on the broiler pan. Broil 5 inches from the heat until the sausage, vegetables, and pineapple are browned, about 4 minutes on each side.

Per serving (1 kebab): 267 Cal, 14 g Fat, 4 g Sat Fat, 68 mg Chol, 658 mg Sod, 22 g Carb, 2 g Fib, 15 g Prot, 7 mg Calc. **POINTS: 6.**

FIVE-STAR TIP If you want to use wooden skewers, be sure to soak them in water for at least 30 minutes to prevent burning. Insert each halfway through the center section of each piece of corn; remove the skewer, then insert it again from the other side so that it goes completely through.

Peppery Turkey Sauté

turkey cutlets
green peppercorns
chicken broth
Worcestershire sauce
frozen mixed vegetables

QUICK LIST

MAKES 4 SERVINGS

This dish gets its kick from green peppercorns—soft, underripe pepper berries that are available in brine or freeze-dried. Green peppercorns have a fresh flavor that's less pungent than black or white peppercorns. We prefer the more assertive taste of green peppercorns packed in brine, which should be drained and rinsed before using, then kept in the refrigerator. Freeze-dried peppercorns can be stored at room temperature in a cool, dark place. Serve the sauté as an entrée with steamed long-grain rice.

1 pound turkey cutlets

1 teaspoon whole green peppercorns, crushed

½ cup fat-free, low-sodium chicken broth

¼ cup white-wine Worcestershire sauce (Worcestershire sauce for chicken)

1 (16-ounce) package frozen mixed vegetable blend, thawed

1. Place the turkey, smooth-side down, between 2 sheets of wax paper and pound to an even ¼-inch thickness with a meat mallet or the bottom of a heavy saucepan.

2. Spray a 12-inch skillet with nonstick spray and set over high heat. Working in batches, if necessary, place the turkey in the skillet and cook until lightly browned, about 2 minutes on each side. Transfer to a large plate.

3. Add the peppercorns and broth to the same skillet and cook, scraping up the browned bits from the bottom of the pan, 20 seconds. Add the Worcestershire sauce and the vegetables; cook 20 seconds. Return the turkey, along with any accumulated juices, to the skillet and cook, stirring frequently, until the sauce reduces to a glaze, 3 minutes. Serve at once.

Per serving (¼ of turkey with ⅔ cup vegetables): 176 Cal, 1 g Fat, 0 g Sat Fat, 82 mg Chol, 306 mg Sod, 11 g Carb, 3 g Fib, 32 g Prot, 40 mg Calc. **POINTS: 3.**

FIVE-STAR TIP   Frozen vegetable blends such as Brussels sprouts, cauliflower, and carrots or cauliflower, carrots, and snow peas would work well in this dish.

Frittata with Sausage,
Red Pepper, and Peas

Frittata with Sausage, Red Pepper, and Peas

QUICK LIST

eggs
turkey sausage links
red bell pepper
onion
peas

MAKES 4 SERVINGS

A classic frittata, an Italian version of an omelette, is cooked open-faced instead of folded over. To reduce the sodium and fat in the sausage, buy the fresh rather than the prepackaged varieties at your favorite supermarket.

6 large eggs
½ teaspoon freshly ground pepper
¼ teaspoon salt
5 ounces fresh turkey sausage links, casings removed and crumbled
½ cup seeded and chopped red bell pepper
1 small onion, chopped
½ cup fresh or thawed frozen peas

1. Preheat the broiler. Whisk the eggs, pepper, and salt in a medium bowl. Set aside.

2. Spray a 10-inch nonstick skillet with nonstick spray and set over medium heat. Add the sausage and brown, breaking it apart with a spoon, about 4 minutes. Drain off any fat. Add the bell pepper and onion; cook until softened, about 3 minutes. Add the peas and cook 30 seconds.

3. Pour the egg mixture into the skillet and reduce the heat to medium-low. Shake the skillet several times so the egg mixture covers the bottom of the pan and the vegetables are evenly distributed. Cover and cook until the top is almost set, about 7 minutes.

4. Wrap the handle of the skillet with foil. Uncover the frittata and place it under the broiler. Broil the frittata until the top is set and firm, about 1 minute. Run a spatula around the edge of the skillet to loosen the frittata and slide it onto a plate.

Per serving (¼ of frittata): 179 Cal, 10 g Fat, 2 g Sat Fat, 334 mg Chol, 527 mg Sod, 6 g Carb, 2 g Fib, 16 g Prot, 46 mg Calc. ***POINTS: 4.***

FIVE-STAR TIP Frittata fillings can be as infinite as your imagination. For even less work, substitute 2 cups corn, broccoli, and red pepper frozen vegetable blend, thawed, for the bell pepper, onion, and peas in this recipe.

QUICK LIST

veal scaloppine
onion
paprika
fat-free sour cream
cholesterol-free egg noodles

Veal Scaloppine with Paprika

MAKES 4 SERVINGS

Inspired by the hearty Hungarian dish, chicken paprikash, this company-friendly entrée is our version of the traditional brown stew thickened with lots of full-fat sour cream. We lighten up matters with fat-free sour cream and take advantage of ultrathin veal scaloppine, which cooks in less than 5 minutes. Avoid bringing the sauce to a boil once you add the sour cream, or it will curdle. Serve with a medley of steamed green beans and carrots.

1 pound thinly sliced veal scaloppine, pounded flat
1 large onion, chopped
2 tablespoons paprika
½ cup water
⅓ cup fat-free sour cream
½ teaspoon salt
½ teaspoon freshly ground pepper
4 cups hot cooked cholesterol-free broad egg noodles

1. Spray a large nonstick skillet with nonstick spray and set over high heat. Working in batches, if necessary, place the veal in the skillet and cook until no longer pink, about 1 minute on each side. Transfer the veal and any juices to a platter and keep warm.

2. Spray the same skillet with nonstick spray and set over medium heat. Add the onion and cook until golden, about 3 minutes. Add the paprika and cook 10 seconds. Add the veal, along with any accumulated juices, and the water. Stir in the sour cream, salt, and pepper and cook, stirring constantly, until just heated through, no more than 30 seconds (do not boil).

3. To serve, divide the noodles in 4 shallow serving bowls. Top each serving with 1 cup of the veal mixture.

Per serving (1 cup each noodles and veal mixture): 378 Cal, 6 g Fat, 2 g Sat Fat, 88 mg Chol, 411 mg Sod, 50 g Carb, 5 g Fib, 32 g Prot, 67 mg Calc. **POINTS: 7.**

FIVE-STAR TIP This dish is also terrific if you substitute one pound turkey scaloppine for the veal—it adds up to the same number of **POINTS.**

QUICK LIST

golden raisins
fresh ginger
capers
dry white wine
sirloin steak

Four-Star Steak

MAKES 4 SERVINGS

We got the inspiration for this simple white-wine sauce from top New York chef Jean-Georges Vongerichten. Its delicate and slightly sour flavor is a good foil to beef. You can also prepare the steak on a ridged grill pan or outdoor grill.

¼ cup golden raisins, chopped

2 tablespoons grated peeled fresh ginger

1 tablespoon capers, drained, rinsed, and chopped

1 (750-milliliter) bottle dry white wine

1 pound sirloin steak, trimmed of all visible fat

½ teaspoon freshly ground pepper

¼ teaspoon salt

1. To prepare the sauce, combine the raisins, ginger, capers, and wine in a medium saucepan and bring to a boil. Reduce the heat and cook at a low boil, stirring occasionally, until the wine mixture reduces to a thin glaze (about ½ cup), about 20–25 minutes.

2. Meanwhile, spray the broiler rack with nonstick spray; preheat the broiler. Sprinkle the steak with the pepper and salt. Broil the steak, 5 inches from the heat, until done to taste, 4–5 minutes on each side for medium-rare. Remove from the heat and let stand 5–10 minutes. Slice the meat and serve with the sauce.

Per serving (3 ounces steak with 2 tablespoons sauce): 209 Cal, 7 g Fat, 3 g Sat Fat, 77 mg Chol, 268 mg Sod, 9 g Carb, 1 g Fib, 27 g Prot, 18 mg Calc. **POINTS: 5.**

FIVE-STAR TIP This sauce would be equally delicious served with 4 (4-ounce) broiled or grilled skinless boneless chicken breasts or 1 (1-pound) pork tenderloin, trimmed of all visible fat. Your tally will come to **3 POINTS** for each chicken breast and **4 POINTS** for each 4-ounce serving of pork.

beef tenderloin
garlic
fennel
canned diced tomatoes
lemon zest

Tuscan Beef Tenderloin

MAKES 4 SERVINGS

Roast beef doesn't have to take hours if you choose the right cut, like succulent tenderloin of beef. To stick to the 30-minute time limit, we quickly prepare the piquant tomato sauce in the same skillet as the roast while the meat stands before carving. (Be careful when preparing the sauce: The handle of the skillet will be very hot, so wear oven mitts or use a sturdy hot pad to hold the pan.)

1 (1-pound) beef tenderloin or filet mignon, trimmed of any visible fat

2 garlic cloves, minced

1 medium fennel bulb, trimmed, halved, and thinly sliced

1 (14½-ounce) can diced tomatoes with Italian herbs

1 tablespoon grated lemon zest

½ teaspoon salt

½ teaspoon freshly ground pepper

1. Preheat the oven to 400°F. Spray a 12-inch nonstick skillet with nonstick spray and set over high heat. Add the beef and cook 3 minutes. Turn the beef over; transfer the skillet to the oven. Roast until the beef reaches an internal temperature of 145°F for medium-rare, 12–15 minutes. Transfer the beef to a cutting board and keep warm.

2. To prepare the sauce, set the same skillet over medium heat. Add the garlic and cook until fragrant, 10 seconds. Add the fennel and cook until softened, about 3 minutes. Add the tomatoes and simmer until slightly thickened, 10 minutes. Stir in the lemon zest, salt, and pepper. Serve the beef with the sauce.

Per serving (¼ of beef with ½ cup sauce): 228 Cal, 9 g Fat, 3 g Sat Fat, 71 mg Chol, 886 mg Sod, 12 g Carb, 2 g Fib, 26 g Prot, 88 mg Calc. **POINTS: 5.**

FIVE-STAR TIP Be forewarned: The beef will smoke quite a bit while roasting, so have good ventilation or a cross-breeze. Serve the dish with mashed or roasted potatoes and/or a colorful mesclun salad.

Tuscan Beef Tenderloin

QUICK LIST

rosemary
oregano
lemon zest
olive oil
rack of lamb

Greek Rack of Lamb

MAKES 6 SERVINGS

Rubbed with a mixture of classic Greek spices, this elegant dish is redolent of the heat-splashed islands of the Aegean. If possible, have your butcher french the racks—or trim all the extra fat around the bones—which makes the chops leaner and gives them a better appearance. However, don't have your butcher cut the chops apart; roast them whole, then slice just before serving.

1½ tablespoons chopped rosemary
1½ tablespoons chopped oregano
1 tablespoon grated lemon zest
½ teaspoon freshly ground pepper
¼ teaspoon salt
2 teaspoons olive oil
2 (¾-pound) racks of lamb (6 ribs each), frenched, and trimmed of all visible fat

1. Preheat the oven to 450°F. Combine the rosemary, oregano, lemon zest, pepper, and salt in a small bowl.
2. Rub the oil onto the meaty sides of the racks, then press the herb mixture onto the meat. Place the racks, meaty-side up, in a baking pan and roast until the lamb reaches an internal temperature of 140°F for medium-rare, 25 minutes. Transfer the racks to a cutting board; cover loosely with foil and let stand 10 minutes. To serve, cut slices between the rib bones.

Per serving (2 ribs): 214 Cal, 11 g Fat, 3 g Sat Fat, 87 mg Chol, 174 mg Sod, 1 g Carb, 0 g Fib, 28 g Prot, 26 mg Calc. **POINTS: 5.**

FIVE-STAR TIP You can roast the lamb for 35 minutes to an internal temperature of 145°F for medium doneness, if desired. Just note that lamb toughens considerably above these temperatures.

5 RULES FOR COOKING QUICK

1. Mise en place. Translation: "Everything in its place." It's every professional chef's golden rule: Place all your ingredients and equipment within arm's length before getting started. That way you won't be wasting time hunting for anything while cooking.

2. Think convenience. Reduce prep time by using precut items like shredded vegetables, packaged salad mixes, and frozen diced onions and vegetable blends (and always use the microwave for thawing).

3. Don't stick around. Always work with nonstick pans and utensils. Not only is this healthier because you'll use less fat, foods will also rotate effortlessly in the pan, saving valuable time.

4. Fire up. Remember, a watched pot never boils. So don't be afraid of high heat to bring a pot of pasta water to a boil (keep the pot covered so it boils even faster), to brown foods, or to reduce a sauce.

5. Clean as you go. Try to keep your workspace as clear of clutter as possible. As soon as you're finished with a utensil or pan, place it in one area of the counter or in the sink. (This will make cleaning up afterward speedier, too.)

Chapter 5

chicken, etc.

great ideas for every part of the bird

QUICK LIST

soy sauce
fresh ginger
star anise
roasting chicken
Asian sesame oil

Asian Roast Chicken with Star Anise and Ginger

MAKES 6 SERVINGS

To trap the succulent juices, we cook a whole marinated bird in a covered roasting pan, then reduce the marinade and add a touch of Asian sesame oil to make a sauce. Notable in this dish is the pungent, bittersweet seasoning, star anise, a star-shaped pod that grows on a small evergreen tree. Often used in Chinese cuisine, it can be found in most supermarkets. (Or, you can substitute ¾ teaspoon crushed anise, fennel seeds, or ground allspice.)

½ cup reduced-sodium soy sauce

½ cup water

2 tablespoons grated peeled fresh ginger

2 star anise

1 (3-pound) roasting chicken

2 teaspoons Asian (dark) sesame oil

1. Combine the soy sauce, water, ginger, and star anise in a large zip-close plastic bag; mix well. Gently loosen the skin from the breast and leg portions of the chicken. Add the chicken to the bag. Squeeze out the air and seal the bag; turn to coat the chicken with the marinade. Refrigerate, turning bag occasionally, at least 8 hours or overnight.

2. Place the oven rack in the lower third of the oven; preheat to 400°F.

3. Spray the rack of a roasting pan with nonstick spray and place in the pan. Tie the legs of the chicken together with kitchen twine and place breast-side up in the roasting pan. Add ½ cup of the marinade to the pan (discard remaining marinade) and cover the pan with foil. Roast until an instant-read thermometer inserted into the thigh registers 180°F, about 1 hour 15 minutes. Transfer the chicken to a cutting board; let stand, covered, 10 minutes.

4. Meanwhile, prepare the sauce: Discard fat from pan drippings. Transfer drippings to a small saucepan (you should have 1 scant cup). Bring drippings to a simmer and cook until the mixture is reduced to ½ cup, about 5 minutes. Stir in the sesame oil.

5. Remove and discard skin from chicken, then carve. Serve with the sauce.

Per serving (⅙ of chicken with about 1 tablespoon sauce): 181 Cal, 8 g Fat, 2 g Sat Fat, 72 mg Chol, 475 mg Sod, 1 g Carb, 0 g Fib, 25 g Prot, 12 mg Calc. **POINTS: 4.**

lemon zest
parsley
garlic
olive oil
chicken

QUICK LIST

Grilled Chicken Gremolata

MAKES 8 SERVINGS

Gremolata is a classic Italian condiment, similar to pesto. Our version boasts the same amount of flavor but only a fraction of the oil. Gremolata can be used with almost any meat, fish, or poultry. If you like, try substituting a combination of citrus zests, such as lemon, orange, and/or lime, for the lemon zest in the recipe. You can also add 1 teaspoon fresh herbs, such as chopped rosemary, thyme, or oregano, for additional flavor.

6 (3 x 1-inch) strips lemon zest
1¼ cups parsley leaves
3 garlic cloves, peeled and sliced
1 tablespoon olive oil
½ teaspoon salt
¼ teaspoon freshly ground pepper
1 (3-pound) chicken, cut into 8 pieces

1. To prepare the gremolata, arrange the strips of lemon zest to form a stack on a cutting board; cut lengthwise into thin slices. Place the parsley and garlic on top of the zest, then chop the mixture until medium-fine. Transfer mixture to a small bowl; stir in the oil, salt, and pepper. Transfer one-third (about 3 tablespoons) of the gremolata to a small bowl; set aside.

2. Gently loosen the skin from the chicken pieces and rub the remaining gremolata evenly under the skin, then rearrange the skin back over the meat to cover.

3. Spray the grill rack with nonstick spray; prepare the grill for indirect heating. Place the chicken, skin-side down, over the indirect heat section of the grill. Cover and grill, turning the chicken every 10 minutes, until cooked through, about 30 minutes.

4. Carefully remove the skin from the chicken, arrange on a platter, and sprinkle with the reserved gremolata.

Per serving (1 piece chicken): 141 Cal, 7 g Fat, 2 g Sat Fat, 54 mg Chol, 205 mg Sod, 1 g Carb, 1 g Fib, 18 g Prot, 26 mg Calc. **POINTS: 3.**

FIVE-STAR TIP To prepare a charcoal grill for indirect heating, arrange hot coals evenly on either side of the charcoal grate. Place a disposable heavy-gauge foil pan in the center of the grate between the coals to collect drippings. Place the chicken on the cooking grate, over the drip pan. To prepare a gas grill, preheat the grill with all burners on high. Then adjust the burners on each side of the food to medium and turn off the burner(s) directly below the chicken.

Roast Chicken with Lemon and Figs

Roast Chicken with Lemon and Figs

lemons
Mission figs
chicken
light brown sugar
balsamic vinegar

QUICK LIST

MAKES 8 SERVINGS

Here's a throw-it-in-the-oven-and-forget-about-it casserole you're sure to prepare again and again. High-fiber, fat-free dried figs, with their dense, sweet flesh and unique crunchy seeds, make a delightful accompaniment to the roasted bird. If you're really fond of lemons, add some extra slices, so there's no fighting over them! (There should be a spare half lemon leftover after juicing.) You may want to serve this dish with ½ cup cooked small pasta, such as orzo, ditalini, or tubetini (for an additional *2 POINTS* per serving).

3 lemons
1 cup dried Mission figs
   (5 ounces)
1 (4½-pound) chicken,
   skinned and cut into
   8 pieces
½ teaspoon salt
¼ teaspoon freshly
   ground pepper
¼ cup packed light
   brown sugar
2 tablespoons balsamic
   vinegar
⅓ cup water

1. Preheat the oven to 400°F. Spray a 9 × 13-inch baking dish with nonstick spray (preferably olive-oil spray).
2. Trim the ends from 1 lemon; cut crosswise into very thin slices (about 12). Place the lemon slices and the figs in the baking dish. Arrange the chicken, skinned-side up, on top; sprinkle with the salt and pepper.
3. Squeeze enough juice from the remaining 2 lemons to equal 3 tablespoons; transfer to a small bowl. Stir in the brown sugar, vinegar, and water. Pour the lemon mixture over the chicken; cover the baking dish loosely with foil.
4. Roast the chicken 35 minutes. Remove the foil and roast, uncovered, basting the chicken twice, until cooked through, 15 minutes more.
5. Transfer the chicken, figs, and lemon slices with a slotted spoon to a serving platter. Discard the fat from the pan drippings; spoon over the chicken.

Per serving (1 piece chicken with 1 tablespoon sauce): 277 Cal, 7 g Fat, 2 g Sat Fat, 81 mg Chol, 234 mg Sod, 25 g Carb, 3 g Fib, 28 g Prot, 64 mg Calc. *POINTS: 6.*

FIVE-STAR TIP   Deep purple-black Mission figs are prized for their luscious moist texture and rich flavor. You can also use tender, golden Calimyrna figs, which have a delicious nutlike flavor, or another variety of dried fruit, such as apricots, peaches, or pears.

QUICK LIST

red onions
rosemary
chicken breasts
unsalted butter
balsamic vinegar

Balsamic Chicken with Caramelized Onions

MAKES 4 SERVINGS

Caramelized onions are a minimalist cook's best friend. Just browning onions with a touch of butter transforms them into a wonderfully sweet, intensely rich condiment for grilled chicken. A splash of tangy balsamic vinegar adds just the right balance to the sweetness of the onions. As a timesaver, you can make and refrigerate caramelized onions for up to two days, then simply reheat in a small skillet or in the microwave.

2 large red onions, halved and thinly sliced

3 teaspoons chopped rosemary

½ teaspoon salt

½ teaspoon fresh ground pepper

4 (6-ounce) skinless boneless chicken breast halves

1½ tablespoons unsalted butter

¼ cup balsamic vinegar

¼ cup water

1. Chop enough of the onions to equal ⅓ cup. Slice the remaining onions and set aside. Combine the chopped onions, 2 teaspoons of the rosemary, ¼ teaspoon of the salt, and ¼ teaspoon of the pepper in a large zip-close plastic bag; add the chicken. Squeeze out the air and seal the bag, press the onion mixture into the chicken to evenly coat. Refrigerate 20 minutes.

2. Meanwhile, melt the butter in a large nonstick skillet over medium heat, then add the reserved sliced onions. Cook, stirring occasionally, until softened and the onions begin to caramelize, 12 minutes. Add the vinegar, water, and the remaining 1 teaspoon rosemary, ¼ teaspoon salt, and ¼ teaspoon pepper. Bring to a simmer and cook, until liquid is almost evaporated and onions are very tender, 5 minutes.

3. Spray a ridged grill pan with nonstick spray; heat pan over medium heat. Remove the chicken from the bag and discard marinade. Grill chicken, turning occasionally, until cooked through, 10–12 minutes. Serve with the onions.

Per serving (1 breast half with ¼ cup caramelized onions): 253 Cal, 8 g Fat, 4 g Sat Fat, 106 mg Chol, 379 mg Sod, 8 g Carb, 1 g Fib, 35 g Prot, 37 mg Calc. *POINTS: 6.*

FIVE-STAR TIP Other sweet onions work nicely here, like Walla Walla or Vidalia—so check your market to see if they're available. You may also substitute fresh thyme or sage for the rosemary, if desired.

Port-Glazed Chicken with Shallots and Dried Cherries

chicken breasts
unsalted butter
shallots
sweetened dried cherries
ruby port wine

QUICK LIST

MAKES 4 SERVINGS

Dried fruit and chicken go beautifully together, especially in this elegant, easy entrée. Light and fruity ruby port wine, dried cherries, and shallots (prized for their mild onion taste) create an intensely flavorful glaze for the chicken. There are a variety of dried fruits you can substitute for the cherries, such as cherry- or orange-flavored sweetened dried cranberries, raisins, or dried plums.

4 (5-ounce) skinless boneless chicken breast halves

¼ teaspoon salt

¼ teaspoon freshly ground pepper

1 tablespoon unsalted butter

¾ pound shallots, halved, if large

⅓ cup sweetened dried cherries

¼ cup water

½ cup ruby port wine

1. Preheat the oven to 375°F. Sprinkle the chicken with the salt and pepper.

2. Melt the butter in a nonstick Dutch oven over medium heat, then add the shallots. Cook, turning occasionally, until they begin to soften and turn golden brown, about 10 minutes. Transfer shallots to a bowl with a slotted spoon and set aside.

3. Add the chicken, skinned-side down, to the same Dutch oven. Cook over medium heat until browned, about 5 minutes. Turn the chicken; add the cherries and water and bring to boil. Scatter the shallots on top and transfer the pot to the oven. Bake, uncovered, until cooked through, 10–12 minutes. Transfer the chicken to a platter and keep warm.

4. Add the port to the Dutch oven. Bring to a boil over medium-high heat and cook until mixture is reduced to a thin glaze, about 5 minutes. Pour glaze over the chicken.

Per serving (1 breast half with about 4 shallots and 1 scant tablespoon glaze): 261 Cal, 6 g Fat, 3 g Sat Fat, 86 mg Chol, 223 mg Sod, 17 g Carb, 2 g Fib, 31 g Prot, 44 mg Calc. **POINTS: 5.**

FIVE-STAR TIP If you need to cut a large shallot in half, leave the root end attached and cut through the root end, so the shallot halves don't fall apart during cooking.

Stuffed Chicken Breasts with Prosciutto and Fontina

MAKES 4 SERVINGS

Lean, skinless boneless chicken breasts are stuffed with Italy's finest ingredients: sweet prosciutto ham, rich and nutty fontina cheese, and fresh basil. We butterfly the chicken in this recipe—a simple technique that's quicker than the traditional method of making a pocket in the meat and placing stuffing inside—to accommodate the filling.

4 (5–6-ounce) skinless boneless chicken breast halves

¼ teaspoon freshly ground pepper

4 (¼-ounce) thin slices prosciutto or lean baked ham

8 large basil leaves

4 tablespoons shredded fontina cheese

2 teaspoons olive oil

1. To butterfly the chicken, place a chicken breast, skinned-side down, on a sheet of wax paper so that one long side faces you. Starting at the thinner end of the breast, begin to cut the chicken lengthwise in half, cutting almost all the way through to the opposite end but still leaving some meat attached. Open up the breast like a book, cover with another sheet of wax paper, and pound to ¼-inch thickness with a meat mallet or the bottom of a heavy saucepan. Repeat with the remaining chicken.

2. Sprinkle the chicken with the pepper. Layer 1 slice of the prosciutto (tuck in the edges of the prosciutto, if necessary, to fit), 2 leaves of the basil, and 1 tablespoon of the fontina over one half of each breast, leaving a ½-inch border. Fold the remaining half of the chicken over to cover the filling, pressing the edges to seal.

3. Heat the oil a large nonstick skillet over medium heat, then add the chicken. Cook until golden-brown and cooked through, 4–5 minutes on each side.

Per serving (1 breast half): 215 Cal, 9 g Fat, 3 g Sat Fat, 91 mg Chol, 295 mg Sod, 0 g Carb, 0 g Fib, 32 g Prot, 53 mg Calc. **POINTS: 5.**

FIVE-STAR TIP Feel free to substitute chopped fresh thyme, rosemary, or sage for the basil. You'll need one teaspoon fresh herbs for each chicken breast half.

Chicken Tenders with Apples and Leeks

QUICK LIST

unsalted butter
chicken tenders
leeks
apples
apple brandy

MAKES 4 SERVINGS

Quick-cooking tenders, the strips of chicken that are attached under the breast, are a great option for busy weeknight dinners. Partnered with apples, leeks, a hint of butter, and apple brandy, they become an elegant, rich-tasting dish. To keep the apples from disintegrating into the sauce, choose a firm yet flavorful variety, such as Granny Smith or Golden Delicious. Serve with a tossed green salad and warm crusty bread.

1½ tablespoons unsalted butter
1 pound chicken tenders
2 leeks, cleaned and sliced
2 apples, peeled, cored, and sliced into thin wedges
⅓ cup water
3 tablespoons apple brandy or regular brandy
¼ teaspoon salt
⅛ teaspoon freshly ground pepper

1. Melt ½ tablespoon of the butter in a large nonstick skillet over medium heat, then add the chicken. Cook, turning occasionally, until lightly colored and cooked through, about 8 minutes. Transfer the chicken to a platter and keep warm.

2. Add the remaining 1 tablespoon butter and the leeks to the same skillet. Cook, stirring occasionally, until the leeks soften, 4 minutes.

3. Add the apples, water, and brandy. Bring to a simmer, cover, and cook until the apples soften but still retain their shape, 6 minutes. Stir in the chicken, salt, and pepper. Cook, until heated through, 2–3 minutes. Serve at once.

Per serving (1¼ cups): 224 Cal, 7 g Fat, 4 g Sat Fat, 74 mg Chol, 209 mg Sod, 16 g Carb, 2 g Fib, 24 g Prot, 42 mg Calc. **POINTS: 5.**

FIVE-STAR TIP   Chicken tenders can be pricey. If you want to use a more economical substitute, cut small skinless boneless chicken breasts in half lengthwise.

QUICK LIST

chicken
canned diced tomatoes
frozen artichoke hearts
kalamata olives
garlic-and-herb feta

Greek-Style Chicken Stew

MAKES 8 SERVINGS

This sensational dish gets its Adriatic flavor from kalamata olives, the dark purple gems of Greece prized for their rich and fruity flavor. Look for kalamatas packed in vinegar, not oil—they're equally delicious. You can skip the feta cheese if you choose and instead add 1 tablespoon chopped fresh oregano during the last three minutes of cooking. Ladle the stew over couscous or steamed spaghetti squash to round out the meal.

1 (3¼–3½-pound) chicken, skinned and cut into 8 pieces
¼ teaspoon salt
½ teaspoon freshly ground pepper
2 (14½-ounce) cans diced tomatoes with basil, garlic, and oregano
1 (9-ounce) package frozen artichoke hearts
12 kalamata olives, pitted and chopped (3 tablespoons)
2 ounces (about ½ cup) garlic-and-herb feta cheese, crumbled

1. Sprinkle the chicken pieces with the salt and ¼ teaspoon of the pepper.
2. Spray a nonstick Dutch oven with nonstick spray (preferably olive-oil spray) and set over medium-high heat. Add the chicken and cook until well browned, 4 minutes on each side. Add the tomatoes, bring to a simmer, and cook 8 minutes.
3. Add the artichoke hearts and olives, stirring until the artichokes are covered with the sauce. Cook until the chicken is cooked through, 12 minutes. Stir in the remaining ¼ teaspoon pepper. Spoon into bowls and sprinkle each serving with the feta.

Per serving (1 piece chicken with ¾ cup vegetables and broth): 229 Cal, 10 g Fat, 3 g Sat Fat, 55 mg Chol, 835 mg Sod, 12 g Carb, 2 g Fib, 22 g Prot, 86 mg Calc. ***POINTS: 5.***

Greek-Style Chicken Stew

QUICK LIST

chicken thighs
Dijon mustard
light brown sugar
lemon juice
fresh bread crumbs

Mustard-Crumb Chicken Thighs

MAKES 4 SERVINGS

Here's a healthy switch from fried chicken, and it's ready to go in a fraction of the time. Tender chicken thighs are coated with a sweet-tart Dijon mixture and dredged in bread crumbs, then broiled until crispy and delicious. The recipe can easily be doubled and served hot or cold—great fixings for a crowd or to serve for a picnic.

1¼ pounds skinless boneless chicken thighs, trimmed of all visible fat

3 tablespoons Dijon mustard

1½ tablespoons packed light brown sugar

1 tablespoon fresh lemon juice

¼ teaspoon freshly ground pepper

¾ cup fresh bread crumbs

1. Place the chicken thighs, skinned-side down, between 2 sheets of wax paper and pound to an even thickness with a meat mallet or the bottom of a heavy saucepan.

2. Combine the mustard, brown sugar, lemon juice, and pepper in a medium bowl. Add the chicken and coat on all sides with the mustard mixture. Cover the bowl with plastic wrap and refrigerate 15 minutes.

3. Meanwhile, spray the broiler rack with nonstick spray; preheat the broiler.

4. Spread the bread crumbs on a sheet of wax paper. Coat the chicken on both sides with the crumbs, gently pressing crumbs to adhere.

5. Place the chicken on the rack. Broil 8 inches from the heat until cooked through and crumbs are golden, about 6 minutes on each side. Cut each thigh in half crosswise and serve at once.

Per serving (about 3 pieces): 280 Cal, 13 g Fat, 3 g Sat Fat, 101 mg Chol, 422 mg Sod, 11 g Carb, 0 g Fib, 29 g Prot, 41 mg Calc. **POINTS: 7.**

FIVE-STAR TIP Substitute your favorite flavored mustard for the Dijon, or an equal amount of honey, jam, or jelly for the brown sugar. Make a batch of fresh bread crumbs (for this recipe, you'll need 1½ slices of bread to make ¾ cup crumbs) for extra-delicious flavor.

Chicken with Chipotle Cream

sour cream
cilantro
lime juice
chipotle en adobo
chicken thighs

QUICK LIST

MAKES 4 SERVINGS

We swear—you'll never guess there's reduced-fat sour cream (not heavy cream) in this smoky grilled chicken slathered with rich, luxurious chile cream sauce! Serve with rice and beans for a terrific south-of-the border meal.

8 tablespoons reduced-fat sour cream

3 tablespoons chopped cilantro

2 tablespoons + 1 teaspoon fresh lime juice

½ large chipotle en adobo, finely chopped, plus 1 teaspoon adobo sauce

¼ teaspoon salt

1¼ pounds skinless boneless chicken thighs, trimmed of all visible fat

1. To prepare the marinade, combine 2 tablespoons of the sour cream, 2 tablespoons of the cilantro, 2 tablespoons of the lime juice, the 1 teaspoon adobo sauce, and ⅛ teaspoon of the salt in a large zip-close plastic bag; add the chicken. Squeeze out the air and seal the bag; turn to coat the chicken. Refrigerate, turning bag occasionally, at least 30 minutes or up to 4 hours.

2. Meanwhile, prepare the Chipotle Cream: Combine the remaining 6 tablespoons sour cream, 1 tablespoon cilantro, 1 teaspoon lime juice, and ⅛ teaspoon salt in a bowl. Stir in ½–1 teaspoon of the chopped chipotle to taste. Cover and refrigerate until ready to serve.

3. Spray the grill or ridged grill pan with nonstick spray; prepare the grill or heat the pan over medium heat. Remove the chicken from the marinade, scraping off any excess. Discard the marinade. Grill the chicken 5 inches from the heat, turning occasionally, until cooked through, 12–16 minutes. Cut each thigh in half crosswise and serve with the Chipotle Cream.

Per serving (about 3 pieces with 2 tablespoons sauce): 263 Cal, 15 g Fat, 5 g Sat Fat, 114 mg Chol, 222 mg Sod, 2 g Carb, 0 g Fib, 29 g Prot, 54 mg Calc. *POINTS: 7.*

Grilled Chicken with
Avocado-and-Corn Salsa

Grilled Chicken with Avocado-and-Corn Salsa

lime juice
cilantro
chicken breasts
fresh corn
avocado

QUICK LIST

MAKES 4 SERVINGS

This is a perfect beat-the-heat summertime meal. The corn zaps in the microwave while the chicken cooks on the outdoor grill, leaving the house nice and cool. The salsa won't burn your taste buds either, because it only needs a pinch of salt, pepper, and splash of lime to taste great. The salsa also makes a fine topper for grilled fish or seafood.

3½ tablespoons fresh lime juice (from 3 limes)

4 tablespoons chopped cilantro

½ teaspoon salt

¼ teaspoon freshly ground pepper

4 (6-ounce) skinless boneless chicken breast halves

2 ears fresh corn

¼ cup water

1 (8-ounce) ripe avocado, peeled and diced

1. Combine 2 tablespoons of the lime juice, 2 tablespoons of the cilantro, ¼ teaspoon of the salt, and ⅛ teaspoon of the pepper in a large zip-close plastic bag; add the chicken. Squeeze out the air and seal the bag; turn to coat the chicken. Refrigerate 20 minutes.

2. Meanwhile, spray the grill rack with nonstick spray; prepare the grill.

3. To prepare the salsa, combine the corn and water in a microwavable dish. Cover and microwave on High until tender-crisp, 3 minutes. When cool enough to handle, cut the corn kernels from the cobs. Combine the kernels with the avocado and the remaining 1½ tablespoons lime juice, 2 tablespoons cilantro, ¼ teaspoon salt, and ⅛ teaspoon pepper in a bowl.

4. Grill the chicken 10 inches from the heat, turning occasionally, until cooked through, 10–12 minutes. Serve with the salsa.

Per serving (1 breast half with ½ cup salsa): 295 Cal, 11 g Fat, 2 g Sat Fat, 94 mg Chol, 378 mg Sod, 14 g Carb, 4 g Fib, 37 g Prot, 25 mg Calc. **POINTS: 6.**

FIVE-STAR TIP   For a smokier flavor, grill the corn for the salsa: Lightly spray the corn with nonstick spray and grill, turning occasionally, until tender, about 6 minutes. Our recipe requires ripe avocado. If only very firm ones are available, speed up the ripening process by placing the fruit in a paper bag and storing at room temperature until ready to eat (usually two to five days). Including an apple in the bag speeds up the process even more.

fat-free yogurt
fresh ginger
cayenne pepper sauce
curry powder
chicken thighs

Chicken Bombay

MAKES 4 SERVINGS

Yogurt-based marinades, like this one spiked with hot pepper sauce, fresh ginger, and curry powder, are great to use with chicken because they both tenderize and infuse the meat with flavor. We like to cook the thighs on an outdoor grill to add a hint of smokiness, but if you're in a hurry, using a ridged grill pan or the broiler works just as well. Serve this dish with a flavored variety of quick-cooking couscous along with steamed carrots and broccoli.

⅓ cup plain fat-free yogurt

1 tablespoon grated peeled fresh ginger

1 tablespoon mild cayenne pepper sauce (e.g., Frank's RedHot Cayenne Pepper Sauce or Crystal's Hot Sauce)

2 teaspoons curry powder

¼ teaspoon salt

8 small skinless boneless chicken thighs (about 1¼ pounds), trimmed of all visible fat

1. To prepare the marinade, combine the yogurt, ginger, pepper sauce, curry powder, and salt in a large zip-close plastic bag; add the chicken. Squeeze out the air and seal the bag; turn to coat the chicken. Refrigerate, turning the bag occasionally, at least 1 hour or overnight.

2. Spray the grill or broiler rack with nonstick spray; prepare the grill or preheat the broiler.

3. Remove the chicken from the marinade, scraping off any excess. Discard the marinade. Grill or broil the chicken 5 inches from the heat, until cooked through, 8–9 minutes on each side.

Per serving (2 thighs): 225 Cal, 12 g Fat, 3 g Sat Fat, 101 mg Chol, 156 mg Sod, 1 g Carb, 0 g Fib, 28 g Prot, 20 mg Calc. *POINTS: 6.*

FIVE-STAR TIP   Not all brands of hot pepper sauce are excessively fiery. We like to use a milder variety in this marinade to allow the ginger and curry flavors to shine through. If you use a sauce that packs significant heat, reduce the amount to two teaspoons.

Spicy Apricot Chicken Drumettes

apricot all-fruit spread
lime juice
fresh ginger
green pepper sauce
chicken drumettes

QUICK LIST

MAKES 4 SERVINGS

Chicken-wing drumsticks (drumettes) are the meaty first section of the wing. They're quick-cooking and great for hors d'oeuvres or for a kid-friendly supper with rice and steamed veggies. Since drumettes are a challenge to skin completely, trim the thicker part of the skin surrounding the meaty section with a small, sharp knife.

½ cup apricot all-fruit spread

3 tablespoons fresh lime juice

3 teaspoons grated peeled fresh ginger

3 teaspoons green pepper sauce

¼ teaspoon salt

2 pounds chicken-wing drumsticks (about 20), trimmed of all visible fat

1. To prepare the marinade, combine the fruit spread, 1 tablespoon of the lime juice, 1 teaspoon of the ginger, 1 teaspoon of the green pepper sauce, and the salt in a small bowl. Transfer 2 tablespoons of the mixture to a large zip-close plastic bag; set the remaining mixture aside for the dipping sauce.

2. Add to the bag the remaining 2 tablespoons lime juice, 2 teaspoons ginger, and 2 teaspoons green pepper sauce; add the chicken. Squeeze out the air and seal the bag; turn to coat the chicken. Refrigerate 20 minutes.

3. Meanwhile, preheat the oven to 425°F. Line a baking sheet with foil and spray with nonstick spray. Place the chicken in a single layer on the baking sheet. Roast until the chicken is cooked through, 20–25 minutes. Serve with the dipping sauce.

Per serving (5 drumettes with 2 tablespoons sauce): 159 Cal, 4 g Fat, 1 g Sat Fat, 46 mg Chol, 223 mg Sod, 12 g Carb, 1 g Fib, 17 g Prot, 71 mg Calc. **POINTS: 3.**

FIVE-STAR TIP   To test the chicken for doneness, insert a small knife into the thicker portion of a drumette—it should no longer be pink near the bone. If you like, you can also use this marinade with skinless boneless chicken thighs.

QUICK LIST

chicken legs
red onions
pale ale
dark brown sugar
thyme

Chicken Legs Braised in Ale

MAKES 4 SERVINGS

Many people prefer the white meat of the chicken, but whole chicken legs—the unseparated drumstick and thigh that are all dark meat—have wonderful flavor and are a great value at the supermarket. This delicious one-pot dish needs little hands-on cooking, and the pale ale (a variety of beer), onions, brown sugar, and thyme impart the chicken with a nutty, complex flavor. If you want to stretch the dish to serve eight, just cut the drumsticks from the thighs before serving.

4 whole chicken legs (about 2 pounds), skinned

¾ teaspoon salt

¼ teaspoon freshly ground pepper

2 large red onions, peeled and cut into 8 wedges each

1 (12-ounce) bottle pale ale

3 tablespoons packed dark brown sugar

2–3 sprigs thyme

1. Sprinkle the chicken with ¼ teaspoon of the salt and ⅛ teaspoon of the pepper.
2. Spray a large nonstick skillet with nonstick spray (preferably olive-oil spray) and set over medium-high heat. Add chicken and cook until browned, 4 minutes on each side; transfer to a plate. Add the onion wedges to same skillet and cook until browned, 2 minutes on each side.
3. Return the browned chicken to the skillet and add the ale, brown sugar, thyme, and the remaining ½ teaspoon salt and ⅛ teaspoon pepper; bring to a simmer. Cover and simmer until cooked through, 20 minutes. Transfer the chicken and the onions to a platter and keep warm.
4. Bring the sauce a boil over high heat. Cook until the sauce is slightly thickened, about 8 minutes. Return the chicken and onions to the skillet. Reduce the heat and simmer until just hot, about 2 minutes more.

Per serving (1 whole leg with ⅓ cup onions and 2 tablespoons sauce): 258 Cal, 9 g Fat, 9 g Sat Fat, 96 mg Chol, 535 mg Sod, 15 g Carb, 1 g Fib, 28 g Prot, 40 mg Calc. **POINTS: 6.**

FIVE-STAR TIP When cutting the onions into wedges, leave the stem end intact so they don't fall apart when cooked. Since this dish simmers for almost 30 minutes, you need not be concerned about the alcohol content; but you can substitute a bottle of nonalcoholic beer for the ale, if desired. Serve this dish with cooked orzo and steamed carrots for a satisfying meal.

chicken drumsticks
cayenne pepper sauce
butter
celery sticks
low-fat blue cheese dressing

QUICK LIST

Buffalo Chicken Drumsticks

MAKES 4 SERVINGS

Legend has it that one day in 1964, Teressa Bellissimo, owner of the Anchor Bar in Buffalo, New York, was faced with having to fix a quick snack for her teenage son and his friends. So she fried a batch of excess chicken wings, dipped them in a buttered spicy chile sauce, and served the wings with celery and blue cheese dressing as a dipping sauce to cut the heat. The result, while delicious, was unfortunately less than healthy—until now. This recipe includes the same components as the original, but instead of the traditional wings, we use skinned chicken legs, which offer more meat and less fat. Add carrot sticks or serve an assortment of packaged precut vegetables to fill out the meal.

8 (about 2¼ pounds) chicken drumsticks, skinned

⅓ cup mild cayenne pepper sauce (e.g., Frank's RedHot Cayenne Pepper Sauce or Crystal's Hot Sauce)

2 tablespoons melted butter or margarine

2 cups celery sticks

½ cup low-fat blue cheese dressing

1. Place the oven rack in the center of the oven; preheat to 425°F.

2. Place the chicken in a shallow 2-quart baking dish; brush with 1 tablespoon of the pepper sauce. Cover the dish with foil and bake until cooked through, 35 minutes.

3. Meanwhile, combine the remaining pepper sauce and the melted butter or margarine in a small bowl. Transfer the chicken to a serving platter; drizzle with 2 tablespoons of the sauce mixture. Serve with the celery, blue cheese dressing, and the remaining sauce.

Per serving (2 chicken legs with ½ cup celery, 2 tablespoons dressing, and 1 generous tablespoon sauce): 288 Cal, 13 g Fat, 5 g Sat Fat, 113 mg Chol, 914 mg Sod, 10 g Carb, 2 g Fib, 30 g Prot, 40 mg Calc. ***POINTS: 6.***

FIVE-STAR TIP   With more hot sauces than ever on supermarket shelves, don't confuse the milder varieties of cayenne pepper sauce with Tabasco sauce from Louisiana. Tabasco peppers are three times hotter than cayenne peppers.

QUICK LIST

chicken cutlets
Caesar dressing
whole-wheat Italian loaf
romaine lettuce
Parmesan cheese

Chicken Caesar Sandwiches

MAKES 4 SERVINGS

Taste the big, bold goodness of a chicken Caesar salad on a roll. No fancy fixins are required for this dish, just quick-cooking chicken cutlets, your favorite Caesar dressing, romaine lettuce, shaved Parmesan, and hearty bread. Use a swivel-bladed vegetable peeler to shave the Parmesan into 1-inch lengths (or substitute 1 ounce freshly grated cheese).

4 chicken cutlets (about 1 pound)

6 tablespoons low-fat Caesar dressing

1 small whole-wheat Italian loaf (about 8 ounces) or 4 (2-ounce) whole-wheat rolls

2 cups sliced romaine lettuce

¼ teaspoon freshly ground pepper

1 ounce shaved Parmesan cheese (¼ cup)

1. Combine the chicken and 2 tablespoons of the dressing in a large zip-close plastic bag. Squeeze out the air and seal the bag; turn to coat the chicken. Refrigerate 20 minutes.

2. Spray a ridged grill pan with nonstick spray; heat the pan over medium heat. Grill the chicken until golden and cooked through, 3½–4 minutes on each side.

3. Split the loaf and cut crosswise into 4 pieces, or split the rolls; layer the bottom half of each with the lettuce and a cutlet. Sprinkle the cutlets with the pepper and drizzle each with 1 tablespoon of the remaining dressing. Top with the Parmesan and remaining bread. Serve at once.

Per serving (1 sandwich): 358 Cal, 12 g Fat, 4 g Sat Fat, 70 mg Chol, 801 mg Sod, 29 g Carb, 3 g Fib, 32 g Prot, 234 mg Calc. ***POINTS: 8.***

FIVE-STAR TIP   If you're using rolls, and they're a bit large, discard enough bread from the centers so that each hollowed-out roll weighs 2 ounces. If the grilled cutlets are much larger than the size of the sandwich, just trim them to fit.

Chicken Caesar Sandwiches

QUICK LIST

hot Italian chicken sausage
escarole
seasoned chicken broth
canned cannellini beans
basil

Chicken Sausage, Escarole, and White Bean Stew

MAKES 4 SERVINGS

How can a five-ingredient stew that takes only 30 minutes to cook taste like it has simmered for hours? By using hot-and-spicy chicken sausage, canned chicken broth seasoned with roasted vegetables, and flavor-packed fresh basil. (We also recommend using olive-oil nonstick spray versus vegetable nonstick spray to boost flavor.) This dish can be prepared and refrigerated for up to two days in an airtight container.

1 pound hot Italian chicken or turkey sausage links (10% or less fat)

1 bunch escarole (about 1 pound), cut crosswise into 1-inch-thick pieces

1 (14½-ounce) can seasoned chicken broth with roasted vegetables and herbs

1 (15½-ounce) can cannellini beans, rinsed and drained

2 cups water

⅓ cup chopped basil

¼ teaspoon freshly ground pepper

1. Spray a large nonstick Dutch oven with nonstick spray (preferably olive-oil spray) and set over medium-low heat. Add the sausage and cook, turning occasionally, until browned and cooked through, about 12 minutes. Transfer to a cutting board; slice when cool enough to handle.

2. Return sausage to the same Dutch oven; add the escarole, broth, beans, and water. Bring stew to a simmer and cook until escarole is just tender, about 10 minutes. Stir in the basil and pepper, remove from the heat, and serve at once.

Per serving (1½ cups): 234 Cal, 10 g Fat, 3 g Sat Fat, 48 mg Chol, 1,220 mg Sod, 16 g Carb, 6 g Fib, 19 g Prot, 87 mg Calc. **POINTS: 5.**

FIVE-STAR TIP   Feel free to use whatever greens look best at the market—Swiss chard, beet greens, and fresh spinach also work beautifully. If you enjoy a smokier taste, try reduced-fat kielbasa instead of the chicken sausage (you'll also save *1 POINT* per serving).

vegetable soup mix
frozen chopped spinach
dry bread crumbs
egg whites
ground chicken

QUICK LIST

Chicken-Spinach Loaf

MAKES 6 SERVINGS

It's hard to believe that any meat loaf could be so tasty with only five ingredients! The secret is packaged vegetable soup mix—that old standby our mothers used to make party dips. Iron-rich spinach also adds great flavor, as well as moisture, to the loaf.

1 (.9-ounce) envelope vegetable soup mix

1 cup boiling water

1 (10-ounce) package frozen chopped spinach, thawed and squeezed dry

½ cup plain dry bread crumbs

½ teaspoon freshly ground pepper

2 egg whites

1½ pounds skinless ground chicken (7% or less fat)

1. Place the oven rack in the center of the oven; preheat the oven to 350°F.

2. Meanwhile, combine the soup mix with the boiling water in a large bowl. Let stand 15 minutes.

3. Combine the spinach, bread crumbs, pepper, and egg whites in a large bowl. Add the chicken and mix until well blended. Place the chicken mixture in the center of a shallow 1½-quart baking dish; form into an 8 × 5-inch loaf. Bake until an instant-read thermometer inserted into the center of the loaf registers 165°F, about 1¼ hours. Let stand 10 minutes before slicing.

Per serving (two ½-inch-thick slices): 187 Cal, 4 g Fat, 1 g Sat Fat, 63 mg Chol, 566 mg Sod, 11 g Carb, 2 g Fib, 27 g Prot, 92 mg Calc. *POINTS: 4.*

FIVE-STAR TIP   Use any leftover loaf for sandwiches, or cut into cubes and stir into prepared marinara sauce for a superquick pasta dinner.

Chicken-and-Bean Chili

chicken thighs
canned diced tomatoes
canned chili beans
green or yellow bell peppers
chipotle en adobo

QUICK LIST

Chicken-and-Bean Chili

MAKES 4 SERVINGS

This smoky-sweet chili gets its kick from chipotles en adobo, dried, smoked jalapeño peppers that are pickled and canned in a tomato-based adobo sauce. Chipotles can be found in Hispanic markets or the ethnic-food section of many supermarkets. Once opened, chipotles keep indefinitely in the refrigerator in an airtight container—a fast fix to zip up your favorite soups and stews. If you want to increase the heat index, add one additional chopped chipotle to the recipe, ½ teaspoonful at a time, to taste.

¾ pound skinless boneless chicken thighs, trimmed of all visible fat, cut into ¾-inch pieces

2 (14½-ounce) cans diced tomatoes with roasted garlic and onion

1 (15½-ounce) can chili beans with seasoning

2 large green or yellow bell peppers, seeded and cut into ¾-inch pieces

1 chipotle en adobo, chopped, plus 1 teaspoon adobo sauce

1. Spray a nonstick Dutch oven or large saucepan with nonstick spray (preferably olive-oil spray) and set over medium-high heat. Add the chicken and cook until browned on all sides, about 6 minutes. Stir in the tomatoes, chili beans, bell peppers, chipotle, and the adobo sauce.

2. Bring the chili to a simmer and cook, stirring occasionally, until the bell peppers are tender and the flavors are blended, about 12 minutes. Serve in bowls.

Per serving (1½ cups): 310 Cal, 9 g Fat, 2 g Sat Fat, 57 mg Chol, 1,540 mg Sod, 36 g Carb, 7 g Fib, 25 g Prot, 82 mg Calc. **POINTS: 6.**

FIVE-STAR TIP For easy dicing, place the chicken thighs in a single layer on a baking sheet lined with plastic wrap. Freeze 40 to 60 minutes, or until just firm, then dice with a sharp knife. For convenience sake, double the amount of chicken, wrap, and freeze half for another batch of chili, for use in stir-fries, or to add to stews.

QUICK LIST

Cornish game hens
apple cider
apple jelly
five-spice powder
cayenne

Apple-Glazed Cornish Game Hens

MAKES 4 SERVINGS

If you haven't tried Cornish game hens, now's the time. These miniature chickens are easy to cook and make great company fare. We broil the hens with their skin so they stay moist and juicy, then remove the skin, slather the meat with a fruity glaze, and broil a few minutes more until bubbly. A dash of five-spice powder (a fragrant blend of cinnamon, cloves, fennel seed, star anise, and Szechwan peppercorns) adds complex flavor to the dish but helps keep the number of ingredients to a minimum.

2 (1½-pound) Cornish game hens, halved
½ cup apple cider
¼ cup apple jelly
1 teaspoon five-spice powder
⅛ teaspoon salt
¼ teaspoon cayenne

1. Spray the broiler rack with nonstick spray; preheat the broiler. Broil the hens 7 inches from the heat, skinned-side down, 15 minutes. Turn the hens and broil until cooked through, 5–10 minutes more.

2. Meanwhile, prepare the glaze: Combine the cider, jelly, five-spice powder, salt, and cayenne in a small saucepan and bring to a simmer. Simmer until the mixture is thick and syrupy, about 7 minutes. Set aside and keep warm. (You should have about ¼ cup.)

3. Carefully remove the skin from each hen. Brush about half of the glaze over the hens. Broil until bubbly, 1–2 minutes more. Place the hens on a serving platter and drizzle with the remaining glaze.

Per serving (½ Cornish hen with about ½ tablespoon glaze): 309 Cal, 7 g Fat, 2 g Sat Fat, 183 mg Chol, 194 mg Sod, 18 g Carb, 0 g Fib, 40 g Prot, 28 mg Calc. **POINTS: 7.**

FIVE-STAR TIP You can substitute 1½ pounds skinned chicken legs (about eight) for the Cornish hens; just increase the cooking time by an additional 5 to 10 minutes (and deduct **2 POINTS** per serving). Serve this autumnal entrée with sautéed cabbage and roasted sweet potato wedges for a satisfying meal.

5 FOOLPROOF SIDE DISHES

Spiced Carrots

MAKES 6 SERVINGS

Cook 1 (16-ounce) bag mini peeled carrots in salted water until the carrots are tender; drain. Rinse under cold water until cool; toss in a large bowl with 2 tablespoons fresh lemon juice, 2 teaspoons extra-virgin olive oil, 1 teaspoon toasted cumin seeds, and $\frac{1}{8}$ teaspoon cinnamon. *1 POINT.*

Guiltless Mashed Potatoes

MAKES 6 SERVINGS

Cook 1 (1$\frac{1}{2}$-pound) bag refrigerated ready-to-cook golden potatoes according to package directions; drain. Meanwhile, microwave $\frac{1}{4}$ cup fat-free chicken broth, 2 tablespoons low-fat milk, and 1 small sprig rosemary in microwavable cup on High until hot. Discard rosemary. Return potatoes to saucepan; coarsely mash with broth mixture, $\frac{1}{2}$ teaspoon salt, and $\frac{1}{4}$ teaspoon pepper. *1 POINT.*

Mexicali Slaw

MAKES 8 SERVINGS

Combine 1 (16-ounce) package coleslaw mix, 2 cups jicama, peeled and cut into thin strips, 1 (4-ounce) can chopped green chiles, drained, $\frac{1}{2}$ cup fat-free ranch dressing, and $\frac{1}{3}$ cup chopped cilantro. *0 POINTS.*

Couscous with Feta and Red Onions

MAKES 4 SERVINGS

Cook 1 (5.7-ounce) package couscous with herbed chicken according to package directions. Meanwhile, heat 1 teaspoon olive oil in a nonstick skillet; add 1 small red onion, chopped, and cook until tender. Fluff couscous with a fork; combine in a large bowl with the onions, 3 tablespoons crumbled reduced-fat feta cheese, and 2 tablespoons sliced toasted almonds. *4 POINTS.*

Fruity Rice

MAKES 4 SERVINGS

Cook 1 cup instant brown rice according to package directions. Stir in 1 (11-ounce) can Mandarin oranges, drained, 1$\frac{1}{2}$ cups peeled, seeded, and chopped cucumber, $\frac{1}{2}$ cup thinly sliced scallions, and $\frac{1}{4}$ cup chopped mint. Serve at room temperature. *3 POINTS.*

Chapter 6

go fish!
smashing seafood entrées

salmon fillet
dry bread crumbs
egg white
Italian seasoning
olive oil

Crispy Salmon Cakes

MAKES 4 SERVINGS

Thanks to the food processor, these salmon cakes are easy to throw together, even on a busy weeknight. (Plus, salmon is often on sale at the supermarket, making this dish a far less expensive option than crab cakes.) Serve these cakes with some lemon wedges or low-fat tartar sauce. They're also terrific when teamed with steamed asparagus and quick-cooking barley for a satisfying dinner.

1 pound skinless boneless salmon fillet, cut into chunks
½ cup plain dry bread crumbs
1 egg white, lightly beaten
1 teaspoon Italian seasoning
¾ teaspoon salt
¼ teaspoon freshly ground pepper
1 tablespoon olive oil

1. Pulse the salmon in a food processor until coarsely chopped. Combine the salmon, bread crumbs, egg white, Italian seasoning, salt, and pepper in a bowl; mix well. Form into 4 (½-inch-thick) cakes.

2. Heat the oil in a large nonstick skillet over medium heat, then add the salmon cakes. Cook until golden and cooked through, 4–5 minutes on each side. Serve at once.

Per serving (1 cake): 215 Cal, 8 g Fat, 1 g Sat Fat, 57 mg Chol, 639 mg Sod, 10 g Carb, 1 g Fib, 24 g Prot, 54 mg Calc. **POINTS: 5.**

FIVE-STAR TIP   When buying salmon from the supermarket, make it one of your last purchases before checking out and always keep it cold. These salmon cakes are great to make ahead. Prepare as directed through Step 1, cover, and refrigerate overnight. Or wrap the uncooked cakes in a double layer of plastic wrap, then in foil, and freeze up to a month. Just be sure to defrost them in the refrigerator overnight, then cook as directed.

flour tortillas
Monterey jack cheese
jumbo lump crabmeat
pickled jalapeño
cilantro

QUICK LIST

Crab Quesadillas

MAKES 4 SERVINGS

Although these quesadillas are anything but ordinary, they couldn't be easier to put together—thanks to the addition of lump crabmeat. Serve with a jicama and watercress salad, or cut each tortilla into six wedges and pass as hors d'oeuvres (for *1 POINT* each).

4 (8-inch) fat-free flour tortillas

1 cup shredded reduced-fat Monterey jack cheese

8 ounces cooked jumbo lump crabmeat, picked over

2 tablespoons pickled jalapeño slices, drained and chopped

4 teaspoons chopped cilantro

1. Arrange 1 tortilla on a work surface. Place 2 tablespoons of the Monterey jack, one-fourth of the crabmeat, 1½ teaspoons of the jalapeño, 1 teaspoon of the cilantro, then 2 tablespoons more of the cheese on half of the tortilla. Fold the tortilla over the filling into a half circle and set aside. Repeat with the remaining ingredients, making a total of 4 quesadillas.

2. Set a large nonstick skillet over medium heat. Add 2 quesadillas and cook until lightly browned and the cheese is melted, 4 minutes on each side. Transfer to a plate and keep warm. Repeat with the remaining 2 quesadillas.

3. To serve, let the quesadillas stand 2 minutes before cutting each in half.

Per serving (1 quesadilla): 241 Cal, 6 g Fat, 3 g Sat Fat, 72 mg Chol, 520 mg Sod, 26 g Carb, 1 g Fib, 23 g Prot, 343 mg Calc. *POINTS: 5.*

FIVE-STAR TIP The recipe works beautifully with a number of fillings. For a vegetarian version, substitute 2 cups sautéed mushrooms with onions and red bell peppers for the crab. Like chicken? Toss in some cooked sliced chicken breast with a little chili powder.

parsley
basil
garlic
extra-virgin olive oil
large shrimp

Grilled Green Shrimp

MAKES 4 SERVINGS

Redolent with the heady flavors of fresh basil and parsley, these herbaceous shrimp are wonderful served alongside grilled veggies or over linguine tossed with olive oil, sautéed garlic, cherry tomatoes, and a little Parmesan cheese.

⅓ cup chopped parsley
⅓ cup chopped basil
2 cloves garlic, minced
4 teaspoons extra-virgin olive oil
¾ teaspoon salt
¼ teaspoon freshly ground pepper
1½ pounds large shrimp, peeled and deveined

1. To prepare the marinade, combine the parsley, basil, garlic, oil, salt, and pepper in a zip-close plastic bag; add the shrimp. Squeeze out the air and seal the bag; turn to coat the shrimp. Refrigerate, turning the bag occasionally, 1 hour or overnight.

2. Spray a nonstick ridged grill pan with nonstick spray and set over medium-high heat. Working in batches, if necessary, grill the shrimp until they are just opaque in the center and lightly browned on the outside, 2–3 minutes on each side.

Per serving (about 9 shrimp): 125 Cal, 3 g Fat, 1 g Sat Fat, 202 mg Chol, 451 mg Sod, 1 g Carb, 0 g Fib, 22 g Prot, 48 mg Calc. ***POINTS: 3.***

FIVE-STAR TIP   Of course, feel free to cook up these tasty jewels of the sea on an outdoor grill for true summertime flavor.

Grilled Green Shrimp

QUICK LIST

extra-large shrimp
extra-virgin olive oil
kosher salt
pepper

Salt-and-Pepper Shrimp

MAKES 4 SERVINGS

This simple technique of cooking the shrimp in their shells adds flavor and helps keep the shrimp moist. It also makes this an interesting and ideal party food to offer at your next buffet. Serve with prepared cocktail sauce, if desired.

1½ pounds extra-large shrimp

1 tablespoon extra-virgin olive oil

1 tablespoon kosher salt

½ teaspoon freshly ground pepper

1. Adjust the racks to divide the oven into thirds; preheat the oven to 450°F. Spray a baking sheet with nonstick spray; set aside.

2. With a sharp pairing knife or small scissors, cut through the back of each shrimp just deeply enough to expose the vein; remove the vein, leaving the shell intact.

3. Combine the shrimp, oil, salt, and pepper in a large bowl; toss well to coat. Arrange the shrimp in a single layer on the baking sheet. Roast on the top oven rack until just opaque in center, 5–7 minutes. Let stand 2 minutes before serving.

Per serving (about 7 shrimp): 133 Cal, 5 g Fat, 1 g Sat Fat, 202 mg Chol, 1,072 mg Sod, 0 g Carb, 0 g Fib, 22 g Prot, 42 mg Calc. *POINTS: 3.*

FIVE-STAR TIP   Kosher salt is preferred by many gourmet cooks because it has a softer flavor than table salt and its coarse grains better adhere to meat, poultry, and fish. Leftovers? Peel and halve the cooked shrimp, then toss with some reduced-fat mayonnaise mixed with a squeeze of fresh lemon juice, and some chopped red onion, celery, and fennel. Serve on multigrain bread or over Boston lettuce leaves.

orange juice
balsamic vinegar
sugar
jumbo sea scallops
olive oil

QUICK LIST

Orange-Glazed Scallops

MAKES 4 SERVINGS

Tender, sweet scallops are one of the most elegant gifts from the sea. Searing them quickly in a skillet keeps them plump and moist on the inside, crisp and golden outside. When selecting scallops, their meat should be nearly translucent and creamy. Avoid wet-looking scallops that have been soaked too long. They will be flimsy, opaque, and will quickly shed a lot of water and weight when cooked.

2 cups orange juice

3 tablespoons balsamic vinegar

1½ tablespoons sugar

1½ pounds jumbo sea scallops (24–30), muscle tabs removed

¾ teaspoon salt

¼ teaspoon freshly ground pepper

1½ tablespoons olive oil

1. To prepare the glaze, combine the orange juice, vinegar, and sugar in a medium saucepan; bring to a boil over medium-high heat. Boil mixture until syrupy and reduced to ¼ cup, 18–20 minutes.

2. Meanwhile, sprinkle the scallops with the salt and pepper. Heat the oil in a large nonstick skillet over medium-high heat. Then, working in batches, if necessary, add the scallops and cook until golden brown on the outside and just opaque in the center, about 3 minutes on each side. Add the glaze and cook, stirring, until scallops are well coated, about 30 seconds. Serve at once.

Per serving (about 6 scallops with 1 tablespoon glaze): 217 Cal, 8 g Fat, 1 g Sat Fat, 27 mg Chol, 597 mg Sod, 21 g Carb, 0 g Fib, 15 g Prot, 39 mg Calc. *POINTS: 5.*

FIVE-STAR TIP   For a great dinner, serve the scallops with snow peas and baby carrots that have been stir-fried with a little garlic and soy sauce, and a side of couscous.

QUICK LIST

pasta sauce
white wine
basil
garlic
mussels

Mussels Provençal

MAKES 4 SERVINGS

Provençal cuisine refers to the dishes of southeastern France—a region where garlic, olive oil, and tomatoes reign supreme. You'll find all these gutsy flavors in this pot of mussels, but to simplify things (and keep the ingredients to a minimum), we use healthful low-fat tomato-basil sauce. To make this a heartier entrée, serve with some crusty bread or spoon a serving of mussels and sauce over 1 cup of your favorite pasta. Either way, you'll want to soak up all the wonderful juices!

1½ cups fat-free traditional pasta sauce

1 cup dry white wine

4 tablespoons chopped basil

3 cloves garlic, minced

1 (2-pound) bag mussels, scrubbed and debearded

1. Heat the tomato sauce in a small saucepan over medium heat; keep warm.

2. Meanwhile, combine the wine, 2 tablespoons of the basil, and the garlic in a large pot; bring to a boil over medium-high heat. Add the mussels, cover, and steam until they open, 5–6 minutes. Discard any mussels that do not open.

3. Divide the mussels into 4 warm bowls; pour half the cooking liquid over the mussels. Spoon the tomato sauce evenly over each serving, then sprinkle with the remaining 2 tablespoons basil. Serve at once.

Per serving (½ pound mussels with about ¾ cup sauce): 218 Cal, 5 g Fat, 1 g Sat Fat, 64 mg Chol, 795 mg Sod, 13 g Carb, 1 g Fib, 28 g Prot, 79 mg Calc. **POINTS: 5.**

FIVE-STAR TIP The hairy filaments that protrude from the mussel are known as a beard. To remove, pinch the filaments between thumb and forefinger and pull firmly. Wait to debeard mussels until as close to cooking time as possible. Reserve the remaining half of the mussel cooking liquid not used in this recipe for a seafood soup or stew. Cool completely and refrigerate up to two days or freeze up to a month.

Near East Marinated Salmon

QUICK LIST
fat-free yogurt
curry powder
garlic
ginger
salmon fillets

MAKES 4 SERVINGS

This tangy, subtly seasoned yogurt marinade wonderfully complements the rich, delicate flavor of salmon. By using skinless fillets, more of the marinade's flavor will permeate the fish (plus, you eliminate extra fat). Serve this dish with a side of lentils and steamed spinach.

⅔ cup plain fat-free yogurt

1 tablespoon curry powder

1 garlic clove, minced

2 teaspoons grated peeled fresh ginger

½ teaspoon salt

¼ teaspoon freshly ground pepper

4 (4-ounce) skinless boneless salmon fillets (1-inch thick)

1. To prepare the marinade, combine the yogurt, curry powder, garlic, ginger, salt, and pepper in a zip-close plastic bag; add the salmon. Squeeze out the air and seal the bag; turn to coat the salmon. Refrigerate, turning the bag occasionally, 4 hours or overnight.

2. Preheat the oven to 450°F. Spray a baking sheet with nonstick spray. Remove the salmon from the marinade and place on the baking sheet. Roast until opaque in the center, 10–12 minutes. Serve at once.

Per serving (1 fillet): 139 Cal, 4 g Fat, 1 g Sat Fat, 57 mg Chol, 230 mg Sod, 2 g Carb, 0 g Fib, 23 g Prot, 45 mg Calc. ***POINTS: 3.***

FIVE-STAR TIP Choose salmon fillets that are moist and free of drying or browning around the edges. The flesh should be firm and spring back when pressed.

Whole Roasted Striped Bass
and Pan Roasted Brussels Sprouts
and Fingerling Potatoes

whole striped bass
extra-virgin olive oil
basil
cilantro
lime juice

QUICK LIST

Whole Roasted Striped Bass

MAKES 8 SERVINGS

Roasting a whole fish is something truly special: Not only does it make a dramatic presentation and enhance the flavor of the fish, but it's also deceptively easy to do. Striped bass, with its medium texture and slightly sweet flavor, is a good candidate for roasting, but you can also try whole red snapper, grouper, or tilapia. For added eye appeal and flavor, serve the bass with Pan Roasted Brussel Sprouts and Fingerling Potatoes [see page 55].

1 (5½–6-pound) whole striped bass, gutted and scaled

1 tablespoon extra-virgin olive oil

1 teaspoon salt

¼ teaspoon freshly ground pepper

⅓ cup chopped basil

¼ cup chopped cilantro

2 tablespoons fresh lime juice

1. Preheat the oven to 500°F. Line a baking sheet with foil and spray with nonstick spray; set aside.
2. With a sharp knife, make 4 deep cuts (down to the bone) crosswise on each side of the bass. Rub the bass with the oil; sprinkle with the salt and pepper.
3. Combine the basil, cilantro, and lime juice in a bowl; rub the mixture on all sides of the bass. Roast until opaque in the center, 45–55 minutes. Transfer the bass to a serving platter.

Per serving (⅛ of fish): 158 Cal, 5 g Fat, 1 g Sat Fat, 117 mg Chol, 391 mg Sod, 1 g Carb, 0 g Fib, 26 g Prot, 26 mg Calc. **POINTS: 4.**

FIVE-STAR TIP When purchasing a whole fish, look for bright, clear eyes, shiny, brightly colored skin, and firm flesh that springs back when pressed with your finger. Whole fish should have a fresh, mild odor and red to bright-pink gills that are free of slime or residue. Most striped bass found in today's fish markets are farm-raised. Wild striped bass, when available, has a slightly more intense flavor with a similar texture.

QUICK LIST

canned diced tomatoes
dry white wine
tomato paste
fennel seeds
grouper fillets

Roast Grouper with Fennel and Tomatoes

MAKES 4 SERVINGS

Grouper is a firm-fleshed fish that's remarkably low in fat. Its sweet, mild taste pairs perfectly with our topping of tomatoes, fennel seeds, and white wine. If grouper is not readily available in your market, catfish, snapper, or halibut fillets make fine substitutes.

1 (14½-ounce) can diced tomatoes with Italian herbs, drained
¼ cup dry white wine
1 tablespoon tomato paste
1 teaspoon fennel seeds, lightly crushed
¾ teaspoon salt
¼ teaspoon freshly ground pepper
1½ pounds skinless boneless grouper fillets

1. Preheat oven to 400°F. Spray a baking sheet with nonstick spray.
2. Combine the tomatoes, wine, tomato paste, fennel seeds, ¼ teaspoon of the salt, and ⅛ teaspoon of the pepper in a bowl.
3. Sprinkle the grouper with the remaining ½ teaspoon salt and ⅛ teaspoon pepper. Place the grouper, skinned-side down, on the baking sheet; top with the tomato mixture. Bake until the grouper is opaque in the center, 15–18 minutes.

Per serving (¼ of grouper with about ⅓ cup tomato mixture): 199 Cal, 2 g Fat, 0 g Sat Fat, 60 mg Chol, 1,071 mg Sod, 10 g Carb, 1 g Fib, 34 g Prot, 99 mg Calc. *POINTS: 4.*

scallions
ginger
soy sauce
honey
halibut fillets

QUICK LIST

Ginger-Steamed Halibut

MAKES 4 SERVINGS

Halibut is a lean, mild-tasting fish that dries out easily when overcooked, so steaming is an ideal way to prepare it. For this recipe, we adapt the French technique, en papillote, which means baking the ingredients inside a parchment parcel. As this fish bakes with fresh ginger, soy sauce, and honey, it creates a moist steam heat, which causes the parcels to puff up. We use foil instead of parchment with equally successful results.

4 scallions, chopped
1 (1-inch) piece peeled fresh ginger, cut into thin strips
2 tablespoons reduced-sodium soy sauce
2 teaspoons honey
4 (6-ounce) skinless boneless halibut fillets

1. Preheat oven to 450°F. Spray 4 (12 × 20-inch) sheets of foil with nonstick spray. Fold the sheets in half from one short end of each sheet.

2. Combine the scallions, ginger, soy sauce, and honey in a small bowl. Unfold the foil. Arrange a fillet on half of each sheet. Top each with one-fourth of the scallion mixture. Fold the foil over the fillets, and crimp the edges, making a tight seal.

3. Place the foil parcels on a large baking sheet and bake until they are puffy, 10–12 minutes. Serve, drizzled with any remaining juices.

Per serving (one parcel): 188 Cal, 3 g Fat, 0 g Sat Fat, 53 mg Chol, 396 mg Sod, 5 g Carb, 0 g Fib, 36 g Prot, 70 mg Calc. **POINTS: 4.**

FIVE-STAR TIP This recipe can be prepared up to three hours in advance. Assemble the parcels as directed, then refrigerate until ready to bake. Because the parcels will be chilled, allow an extra 2 to 3 minutes of baking time to fully cook the fish.

QUICK LIST

mayonnaise
tarragon
tuna steaks
French baguette
baby greens

Grilled Tuna on Baguette

MAKES 4 SERVINGS

Fresh tuna steaks make great sandwiches—especially when they're grilled and slathered with tarragon mayo. When purchasing fresh tuna, look for bright red, shiny flesh. The steaks should also be firm and have no bruises or tears.

¼ cup reduced-fat mayonnaise

½ teaspoon dried tarragon

4 (4-ounce) tuna steaks (½-inch thick)

½ teaspoon salt

¼ teaspoon freshly ground pepper

1 (8-ounce) French baguette, split in half lengthwise and quartered

1 cup loosely packed baby greens

1. Combine the mayonnaise and tarragon in a small bowl and set aside.

2. Sprinkle the tuna with the salt and pepper. Spray a nonstick ridged grill pan with nonstick spray and set over medium-high heat. Grill the tuna until just pink in the center, 3–4 minutes on each side.

3. Meanwhile, split the baguette and cut crosswise into 4 pieces. Place one-fourth of the greens on the bottom half of each baguette. Top each with a tuna steak; spread each steak with 1 tablespoon of the mayonnaise mixture. Top with the remaining baguette halves.

Per serving (1 sandwich): 413 Cal, 12 g Fat, 2 g Sat Fat, 54 mg Chol, 794 mg Sod, 44 g Carb, 4 g Fib, 31 g Prot, 36 mg Calc. *POINTS: 8.*

QUICK LIST

rice vinegar
honey
Asian sesame oil
tuna steaks
sesame seeds

Tuna Steaks with Sesame Crust

MAKES 4 SERVINGS

A simple, easy crust adds lots of flavor to tuna without a ton of work. This recipe can be served straight out of the pan or enjoyed later at room temperature. To make an entrée salad, try serving the steaks over Asian greens tossed with some of the vinaigrette dressing.

3 tablespoons rice vinegar

2 tablespoons honey

1 tablespoon Asian (dark) sesame oil

¾ teaspoon salt

¼ teaspoon freshly ground pepper

4 (6-ounce) tuna steaks (½-inch thick)

2 tablespoons sesame seeds

1. To prepare the vinaigrette, combine the vinegar, honey, sesame oil, ¼ teaspoon of the salt, and ⅛ teaspoon of the pepper in a small bowl.

2. Sprinkle both sides of tuna with the remaining ½ teaspoon salt and ⅛ teaspoon pepper. Spread the sesame seeds on a plate; add the tuna, gently pressing both sides into the seeds to coat evenly.

3. Spray a large nonstick skillet with nonstick spray and set over medium-high heat. Add the tuna and cook until done to taste, 3–4 minutes on each side for medium-rare. Drizzle the vinaigrette on top of each serving.

Per serving (1 tuna steak with 1½ tablespoons vinaigrette): 263 Cal, 7 g Fat, 1 g Sat Fat, 74 mg Chol, 499 mg Sod, 10 g Carb, 1 g Fib, 39 g Prot, 34 mg Calc. *POINTS: 6.*

FIVE-STAR TIP   For an extra-flavorful crust, toast the sesame seeds in a dry skillet over medium-low heat. Cook, shaking the pan and stirring constantly, until fragrant. Watch them carefully; sesame seeds can burn quickly. Transfer the seeds to a plate to cool.

QUICK LIST

Dijon mustard
marjoram
garlic
extra-virgin olive oil
swordfish steaks

Marjoram-Scented Swordfish

MAKES 4 SERVINGS

Marjoram is an ancient herb and a member of the mint family. Its pale green leaves resemble those of oregano and have a similar yet slightly more floral flavor. Marjoram balances beautifully with the full flavor of swordfish, and both are perfect for grilling. This dish pairs nicely with our Snappy Fig and Arugula Salad [see page 164].

3 tablespoons Dijon
mustard
2 tablespoons chopped
fresh marjoram or
2 teaspoons dried
2 cloves garlic, minced
1 tablespoon extra-virgin
olive oil
½ teaspoon salt
¼ teaspoon freshly
ground pepper
4 (6-ounce) swordfish
steaks

1. To prepare the marinade, combine the mustard, marjoram, garlic, oil, salt, and pepper in a zip-close plastic bag; add the swordfish. Squeeze out the air and seal the bag; turn to coat the swordfish. Refrigerate, turning the bag occasionally, 30 minutes or overnight.

2. Spray a nonstick ridged grill pan with nonstick spray and set over medium-high heat. Grill the swordfish until browned on the outside and opaque in the center, 4 minutes on each side. Serve at once.

Per serving (1 steak): 164 Cal, 7 g Fat, 2 g Sat Fat, 45 mg Chol, 392 mg Sod, 1 g Carb, 0 g Fib, 24 g Prot, 18 mg Calc. ***POINTS: 4.***

FIVE-STAR TIP Marjoram is also wonderful with tuna steaks, salmon and snapper fillets, as well as pork tenderloin and skinless boneless chicken thighs.

Marjoram-Scented Swordfish and
Snappy Fig and Arugula Salad

QUICK LIST

cod fillets
olive oil
lemon and pepper seasoning
lemon zest
salt

Lemon-Pepper Cod

MAKES 4 SERVINGS

Cod has been one of the most important varieties of fish for the Northeast economy since the time of the first settlers. So revered was cod that its name was given to one of New England's most famous communities, Cape Cod. With its mild taste and delicate texture, cod is a great choice for baking, broiling, or sautéing.

4 (6-ounce) skinless
  boneless cod fillets
4 teaspoons olive oil
1½ teaspoons lemon and
  pepper seasoning
  (no salt added)
2 teaspoons grated
  lemon zest
¾ teaspoon salt

1. Preheat oven to 350°F. Spray a baking sheet with nonstick spray.
2. Place the cod, skinned-side down, on the baking sheet. Brush the tops with the oil and sprinkle with the lemon and pepper seasoning, lemon zest, and salt. Bake until opaque in the center, 10–12 minutes.

Per serving (1 fillet): 127 Cal, 5 g Fat, 1 g Sat Fat, 45 mg Chol, 500 mg Sod, 1 g Carb, 0 g Fib, 19 g Prot, 16 mg Calc. **POINTS: 3.**

FIVE-STAR TIP   Other regional names for cod include rock cod, codling, and scrod. This recipe also works well with flounder or sole fillets.

Mojo-Marinated Snapper

orange juice
lime juice
cilantro
garlic
red snapper fillets

QUICK LIST

MAKES 4 SERVINGS

Mojo is a traditional Cuban marinade that calls for sour orange juice—a very difficult ingredient to find. So we've substituted fresh orange juice along with tangy lime juice with great success. We leave the skin on the snapper, which becomes nicely crisp when grilled and helps the fish stay moist. If you prefer, remove it before serving and save *1 POINT*. This speedy marinade also works well with catfish, grouper, or sea bass fillets.

⅓ cup fresh orange juice

3 tablespoons fresh lime juice

¼ cup chopped cilantro

3 cloves garlic, minced

4 (6-ounce) red snapper fillets, with skin

1 teaspoon salt

¼ teaspoon freshly ground pepper

1. To prepare the marinade, combine the orange juice, lime juice, cilantro, and garlic in a zip-close plastic bag; add the snapper. Squeeze out the air and seal the bag; turn to coat the snapper. Refrigerate, turning the bag occasionally, 30 minutes.

2. Remove the snapper from the marinade; sprinkle with the salt and pepper.

3. Spray a nonstick ridged grill pan with nonstick spray and set over medium-high heat. Place the snapper, skin-side up, in the pan and grill, turning once, until opaque in the center and the skin is crisp, 14–16 minutes.

Per serving (1 fillet): 119 Cal, 2 g Fat, 0 g Sat Fat, 42 mg Chol, 633 mg Sod, 1 g Carb, 0 g Fib, 24 g Prot, 39 mg Calc. *POINTS: 3.*

Pan-Fried Catfish

MAKES 4 SERVINGS

Farmed-raised catfish is a great value and widely available at your supermarket fish counter. Catfish's firm texture and sweet, slightly rich flavor make it ideal for pan-frying, especially when served with a dollop of Old Bay-seasoned mayonnaise. Old Bay seasoning—a blend of celery, bay leaves, mustard, cayenne, and ginger—is traditionally used for crab cakes and was once a staple enjoyed only by a lucky few along the Chesapeake Bay. Today, it's readily available at the supermarket for anyone who wishes to experience its distinctive big, bold taste.

⅓ cup fat-free mayonnaise

1½ tablespoons fresh lemon juice

¾ teaspoon Old Bay seasoning

4 (6-ounce) skinless boneless catfish fillets

¾ teaspoon salt

¼ teaspoon freshly ground pepper

1 tablespoon canola oil

1. To prepare the Old Bay mayonnaise, combine the mayonnaise, lemon juice, and Old Bay seasoning in a small bowl; set aside.

2. Sprinkle the catfish with the salt and pepper. Heat a large nonstick skillet over medium-high heat. Swirl in the oil, then add the catfish. Cook until just opaque in the center, about 3 minutes on each side.

3. Transfer the catfish to 4 serving plates, and top each serving with the mayonnaise.

Per serving (1 fillet with 1½ tablespoons mayonnaise): 257 Cal, 17 g Fat, 4 g Sat Fat, 76 mg Chol, 469 mg Sod, 5 g Carb, 0 g Fib, 26 g Prot, 1 mg Calc. *POINTS: 7.*

FIVE-STAR TIP   Serve this fish with your favorite coleslaw and some warm corn bread for a true taste of the South.

tilapia fillets
extra-virgin olive oil
garlic
capers
canned diced tomatoes

QUICK LIST

Tilapia Italiano

MAKES 4 SERVINGS

Tilapia is a firm, flaky fish that has a pleasantly sweet, mild flavor. Also low in fat, it's farm-raised, and thus widely available. Tilapia is an ideal fish to serve with this flavorful caper-tomato sauce, along with warm, crunchy rolls and a crisp green salad.

4 (6-ounce) skinless
  boneless tilapia fillets
¾ teaspoon salt
¼ teaspoon freshly
  ground pepper
4½ teaspoons extra-virgin
  olive oil
3 cloves garlic, minced
1 tablespoon capers,
  drained
1 (14½-ounce) can
  diced tomatoes with
  Italian herbs

1. Sprinkle the tilapia with ½ teaspoon of the salt and ⅛ teaspoon of the pepper. Heat 2 teaspoons of the oil in a large nonstick skillet over medium-high heat, then add the tilapia. Cook until just opaque in the center, 2–3 minutes on each side. Transfer the fish to a platter and keep warm.
2. Return the skillet to the heat. Add the remaining 2½ teaspoons oil, then add the garlic and capers. Cook until fragrant, 30 seconds. Add the tomatoes and the remaining ¼ teaspoon salt and ⅛ teaspoon pepper. Cook until the tomato mixture starts to thicken, 3–4 minutes. Add the tilapia and cook until heated through, about 1 minute longer. Serve at once.

Per serving (1 fillet with ¼ cup sauce): 198 Cal, 6 g Fat, 1 g Sat Fat, 64 mg Chol, 1,075 mg Sod, 10 g Carb, 1 g Fib, 25 g Prot, 71 mg Calc.
POINTS: 4.

FIVE-STAR TIP   This Mediterranean-style sauce would also pair perfectly with rockfish, walleye, pike, or orange roughy fillets.

The Complete Cupboard

Can't make a dish because you're missing an ingredient? Have these staples on hand and you'll be ready to cook at a moment's notice.

In the Pantry
Asian hot chili sauce
Bread crumbs (fresh, plain dried)
Brown sugar (dark, light)
Canned and dried beans (black, cannellini, chickpeas, kidney, pink, white)
Canned chicken broth (fat-free, low-sodium, roasted vegetables and herbs)
Canned diced tomatoes (flavored with green chiles, roasted garlic, Italian herbs, jalapeños, and onion)
Canned whole tomatoes in juice
Capers
Chipotle en adobo
Couscous
Dried fruit (apricots, sweetened dried cherries, cranberries, currants, golden raisins, Mission figs)
Instant polenta
Lentils (brown, green)
Marinara sauce
Mustard (Dijon, honey)
Noodles (bean-thread, broad cholesterol-free egg, lo mein, rice-stick, somen)
Oil (Asian [dark] sesame, canola, garlic, olive, extra-virgin olive)
Onions, scallions, garlic, shallots
Pasta (campanile, capellini, cavatappi, fettuccini, gemelli, linguine, mostaccioli, orecchiette, penne, radiatore, rigatoni, shells, trumpetti, ziti)
Pepper sauce (cayenne [mild], green)
Potatoes (red, Yukon Gold)
Prepared salsa (roasted tomatillo, salsa verde)
Reduced-sodium soy sauce
Rice (basmati, Texmati, long-grain white, seasoned rice mix)
Spices (cayenne, ground ancho chile, curry powder, fennel seeds, five-spice, garlic powder, hot and smoked paprika, crushed red pepper, saffron, sesame seeds, star anise, Jamaican jerk seasoning, Mexican spice blend)

Sun-dried tomatoes (not oil-packed)
Thai red curry paste
Tomato paste
Vinegar (balsamic, cider, red-wine, sherry, white-wine)
Tuna (water-packed canned)
Wine and spirits (red, dry white, and ruby port wines; dry sherry; vermouth; apple brandy)

In the Fridge

Assorted salad dressings (creamy dill, low-fat blue cheese, low-fat Caesar, low-fat vinaigrette, low-fat ginger vinaigrette, fat-free poppy seed)
Bagged rinsed baby greens, baby spinach
Bell pepper (green, red, yellow)
Cheese (reduced-fat cheddar, farmer, feta, fontina, goat, reduced-fat Gruyère, reduced-fat Monterey jack, fat-free mozzarella, Parmesan)
Chiles (Fresno, jalapeño, poblano, serrano, Thai)
Eggs
Ginger (fresh)
Herbs (fresh and/or dried basil, cilantro, dill, marjoram, mint, oregano, parsley, rosemary, sage, thyme)
Lemons, limes, oranges
Mayonnaise (fat-free, reduced-fat)
Mushrooms (cremini, shiitake, white)
Olives (marinated black with herbs, kalamata)
Pizza crust (thin, prebaked)
Sour cream (fat-free, reduced-fat)
Tofu
Tortilla
Yogurt (plain, fat-free and low-fat)

In the Freezer

Shrimp
Mixed vegetable blends
Vegetables (corn, sliced okra, peas, chopped spinach)

Chapter 7

the heat is on

fiery favorites (but not *too* hot)

Snappy Fig and Arugula Salad

MAKES 6 SERVINGS

This recipe is a delicious example of how just a few, superflavorful ingredients can make a big impact. The stylish salad features tangy balsamic vinaigrette, sweet dried figs, and smoky-hot chipotle chile—all tossed with peppery arugula leaves. Serve alone or as a side salad with simple grilled fish, chicken, or steak.

¼ cup balsamic vinaigrette dressing

1 cup (about 15) dried Mission figs, halved

1 medium shallot, minced (about 2 tablespoons)

1 chipotle en adobo, finely chopped

½ teaspoon salt

¼ teaspoon freshly ground pepper

2 (6–8-ounce) bunches arugula, trimmed

1. To prepare the dressing, microwave the vinaigrette dressing in a small microwavable bowl on High until hot but not boiling, about 30 seconds. Add the figs, shallot, chipotle, salt, and pepper; let stand 30 minutes.
2. Combine the arugula with the dressing in a large bowl. Toss well and serve at once.

Per serving (about 1 cup): 145 Cal, 5 g Fat, 1 g Sat Fat, 0 mg Chol, 322 mg Sod, 25 g Carb, 5 g Fib, 2 g Prot, 115 mg Calc. **POINTS: 3.**

FIVE-STAR TIP   The dressing can be prepared and refrigerated a day ahead. Just return it to room temperature before tossing with the greens for maximum taste.

Peppery Pizza with Greens

broccoli rabe
olive oil
garlic
crushed red pepper
pizza crust

QUICK LIST

MAKES 6 SERVINGS

Gutsy and full of flavor, this pie should please die-hard pizza fans. Broccoli rabe has a slightly peppery bite, which is accentuated by a good pinch of crushed red pepper. If you're willing to up the ingredient count to six, sprinkle the top with ½ cup part-skim mozzarella, but you'll also have to add another **_POINT_** per serving.

1 large (1-pound) bunch
 broccoli rabe, trimmed
1 tablespoon olive oil
2 large garlic cloves,
 crushed through a press
½ teaspoon crushed
 red pepper
1 (10-ounce) package thin
 pizza crust

1. Preheat the oven to 450°F. Put the broccoli rabe in a steamer basket; set in a large saucepan over 1 inch of boiling water. Cover tightly and steam until bright green and tender-crisp, 5–6 minutes. When the broccoli rabe is cool enough to handle, coarsely chop and set aside.
2. Discard the water and wipe out the same saucepan; heat over medium heat. Add the oil, then add the garlic and crushed red pepper. Cook the garlic until fragrant, about 30 seconds. Add the broccoli rabe and cook until very tender, 5–6 minutes more.
3. Place the pizza crust on a baking sheet. Spread the broccoli rabe mixture on the crust. Bake until hot and browned on the bottom, 12–14 minutes. To serve, slide the pizza onto a large cutting board, then cut into 6 slices.

Per serving (1 slice): 159 Cal, 5 g Fat, 1 g Sat Fat, 0 mg Chol, 262 mg Sod, 24 g Carb, 1 g Fib, 7 g Prot, 144 mg Calc. **_POINTS: 3._**

QUICK LIST

falafel mix
light mayonnaise
chipotle en adobo
whole-wheat pitas
romaine lettuce

Fiery Falafel

MAKES 8 SERVINGS

Falafel is a classic Middle Eastern sandwich that usually consists of spicy deep-fried chickpea balls topped with yogurt sauce and wrapped in pita bread. For this recipe, we skip the deep-frying, take advantage of convenient prepared falafel mix, and substitute zesty chipotle mayonnaise for the yogurt.

1 (10-ounce) package falafel mix

1¼ cups water

6 tablespoons light mayonnaise

2 teaspoons minced chipotle en adobo

4 teaspoons olive oil

4 onion or whole-wheat pitas, cut crosswise in half

8 large romaine lettuce leaves, ribs removed and cut in half

1. Combine the falafel mix and the water and let stand according to package directions.

2. Meanwhile, combine the mayonnaise and chipotle in a small bowl; set aside.

3. Drop the falafel mixture by 2-tablespoon measures onto a large sheet of wax paper. (You should have 20 mounds.)

4. Heat 1 teaspoon of the oil in a 12-inch nonstick skillet over medium-high heat. Quickly shape 5 mounds of the falafel mixture into 2-inch patties and add to the skillet. Cook until the patties are golden and firm, 1½–2 minutes on each side. Transfer the patties to a plate and keep warm. Repeat 3 more times with the remaining falafel mixture and the oil, using 1 teaspoon of the oil to cook each batch.

5. Spread the inside of each pita half with 1½ teaspoons of the chipotle mayonnaise. Cut 4 of the falafel patties in half. Fill each pita half with 2½ falafel patties and ½ lettuce leaf. Serve at once.

Per serving (½ falafel): 251 Cal, 8 g Fat, 1 g Sat Fat, 4 mg Chol, 861 mg Sod, 37 g Carb, 8 g Fib, 14 g Prot, 58 mg Calc. ***POINTS: 5.***

onions
chicken broth
hot paprika
Gruyère cheese
phyllo pastry shells

QUICK LIST

Spicy Onion Tartlets

MAKES 30

If you love to entertain, miniature phyllo shells are a great item to have stashed in the freezer. These elegant little gems can be filled with just about anything—like this deceptively simple yet tasty mix of caramelized onions, hot paprika, and grated cheese. Best of all, these spicy bites can be made several hours ahead, kept at room temperature, then baked to order.

2 medium-large sweet onions, such as Vidalia, cut into very thin wedges (about 1¾ pounds)

2 tablespoons low-sodium chicken broth or water

½–¾ teaspoon hot paprika (preferably Hungarian)

¼ teaspoon salt

⅓ cup coarsely grated reduced-fat Gruyère or Jarlsberg cheese

2 (2.1-ounce) packages frozen mini phyllo pastry shells

1. To prepare the filling, spray a 12-inch nonstick skillet with nonstick spray and set over medium heat. Add the onions, cover, and cook until the onions are tender and have released their liquid, 10–12 minutes. Uncover and cook until the onions are golden, 30 minutes. Stir in the broth, paprika, and salt; cook until the broth has evaporated and the onions are very tender, 3–4 minutes more. (You should have 2¾ cups.) Cool 15 minutes.

2. Meanwhile, preheat the oven to 350°F.

3. Stir the Gruyère into the cooled filling. Place the pastry shells on a baking sheet; spoon a level 1½ teaspoons filling into each shell. Bake until the pastry is lightly crisped and the filling is hot, 6–8 minutes. Serve at once.

Per serving (1 tartlet): 38 Cal, 1 g Fat, 0 g Sat Fat, 1 mg Chol, 35 mg Sod, 5 g Carb, 1 g Fib, 1 g Prot, 17 mg Calc. **POINTS: 1.**

FIVE-STAR TIP Caramelizing is a process that should not be rushed, because the rich, complex sweetness of onions relies on gentle cooking. First, the onions need to deflate in volume and become tender and translucent before the browning begins. (If the onions begin to brown too quickly, reduce the heat.) However, if the onions have a high moisture content and are not browning during the last 20 minutes of the cooking time, increase the heat slightly.

Mini Red-Curry Burgers

| zucchini |
| ground beef |
| onion |
| Thai red curry paste |
| low-fat yogurt |

QUICK LIST

Mini Red-Curry Burgers

MAKES 4 SERVINGS

Thai red curry paste—a blend of red chiles, garlic, onion, lemongrass, spices, and shrimp paste—not only adds heat but also great flavor to ground beef, eliminating the need to use lots of other ingredients. Thai curry paste can be found in jars or foil packets in the ethnic-food section of the supermarket. Grated zucchini adds both moisture to the patties and a mellow flavor to the cool yogurt sauce.

1 medium zucchini

¾ pound lean ground beef (10% or less fat)

2 tablespoons + 1 teaspoon grated onion

½ teaspoon + ⅛ teaspoon salt

2 teaspoons Thai red curry paste

⅓ cup plain low-fat yogurt

1. Coarsely shred the zucchini; set aside ⅓ cup.
2. Combine the remaining zucchini, the beef, 2 tablespoons of the onion, ½ teaspoon of the salt, and the curry paste in a bowl. Form into 8 (2½-inch) burgers.
3. Spray a large nonstick skillet with nonstick spray and set over medium-high heat. Add 4 of the burgers and cook until the meat is done to taste, 3–4 minutes on each side for medium. Set aside and keep warm. Repeat with the remaining burgers.
4. Meanwhile, prepare the yogurt sauce: Combine the yogurt, the reserved ⅓ cup zucchini (save a bit for garnish, if desired), and the remaining 1 teaspoon onion and ⅛ teaspoon salt in a small bowl. Serve with the burgers.

Per serving (2 burgers with 2 tablespoons sauce): 115 Cal, 4 g Fat, 0 g Sat Fat, 38 mg Chol, 476 mg Sod, 4 g Carb, 1 g Fib, 15 g Prot, 46 mg Calc. *POINTS: 2.*

FIVE-STAR TIP   Serve the burgers with pita wedges, as well as a dark green salad of romaine, bell pepper strips, radishes, and cucumbers (or any other precut veggies from the salad bar).

QUICK LIST

stewed tomatoes
Spanish smoked paprika
baby spinach
canned chickpeas
salt

Smoky Spinach and Chickpea Stew

MAKES 4 SERVINGS

Paprika is made by grinding aromatic sweet red pepper pods, although some varieties are very hot. For this stew we use Spanish paprika, *pimentón*, which is uniquely smoked, thus producing an extraordinary flavor. All supermarkets carry mild paprika, but you have to head to ethnic markets to find the more pungent varieties. If Spanish smoked paprika is not available in your area, substitute hot paprika. Serve this dish over quick-cooking couscous or any other grain.

1 (15-ounce) can stewed
  tomatoes
½–1 teaspoon smoked
  Spanish paprika
2 (7–8-ounce) bags baby
  spinach, or 1 large
  (1-pound) bunch spinach
1 (15½-ounce) can
  chickpeas (garbanzo
  beans), rinsed and
  drained
½ teaspoon salt

Combine the tomatoes and paprika in a Dutch oven or 4-quart saucepan and bring to a boil over medium-high heat; boil 1 minute. Add the spinach; cover and cook until the spinach wilts, 3–4 minutes. Stir in the chickpeas and salt. Cover, reduce the heat, and cook until the spinach is just tender and the flavors are blended, about 4 minutes more.

Per serving (¼ of stew): 120 Cal, 2 g Fat, 0 g Sat Fat, 0 mg Chol, 659 mg Sod, 23 g Carb, 7 g Fib, 7 g Prot, 157 mg Calc. ***POINTS: 2.***

FIVE-STAR TIP You can also substitute an equal amount of minced chipotle chile en adobo for the paprika.

| dried cannellini beans |
| vegetable broth |
| sage |
| red Jalapeño |
| butternut squash |

QUICK LIST

Chile, Bean, and Butternut Squash Stew

MAKES 4 SERVINGS

If you love hot food, most likely you're familiar with green jalapeño chiles, which pack a good amount of heat and flavor. Come autumn, keep an eye open for red jalapeños, a variety that's even hotter than their green cousins! Creamy white cannellini beans and sweet roasted butternut squash tastefully tame the heat. Serve this dish with crusty bread and a green salad for a hearty, healthy meal.

½ pound dried cannellini beans, picked over, rinsed, and drained

1 (14½-ounce) can vegetable broth

1 cup water

8–10 sage leaves, thinly sliced

1 red jalapeño or red Fresno chile, seeded and minced (wear gloves to prevent irritation)

½ teaspoon salt

1 (1-pound) butternut squash, peeled and diced

1. Soak the beans according to package directions.

2. Combine the soaked beans, broth, and water in a large saucepan and bring to a boil. Reduce the heat, cover, and cook at a low boil until the beans are almost tender, 30–40 minutes. Add the sage, chile, and salt; cover and simmer until the beans are tender but still hold their shape and the cooking liquid just covers the beans, 15–25 minutes.

3. Meanwhile, preheat the oven to 450°F. Spray the broiler rack with nonstick spray. Place the squash on the rack in a single layer; spray with nonstick spray. Roast until the squash is golden brown and tender, 15 minutes.

4. Stir the squash into the beans. Serve at once.

Per serving (1¼ cups): 232 Cal, 4 g Fat, 0 g Sat Fat, 0 mg Chol, 740 mg Sod, 41 g Carb, 11 g Fib, 12 g Prot, 89 mg Calc. **POINTS: 4.**

FIVE-STAR TIP Fresno chiles are similar to jalapeños, except they tend to be thinner. You may also use serrano or fresh cayenne chiles as a substitute. To prepare the dish ahead, cool completely and refrigerate in an airtight container up to two days.

QUICK LIST

dried pink beans
olive oil
onion
chicken broth
chipotle en adobo

Hot-and-Smoky Pink Beans

MAKES 12 SERVINGS

One taste of this creamy bean dish and you'll never miss the refried version again! We actually get away with using only a smidgen of oil—thanks to cooking the beans with a generous amount of sweet browned onions, then adding a shot of chipotle chile to the mix just before serving. Serve the beans with brown rice and steamed spinach and you've got a complete vegetarian meal.

1 pound dried pink beans, picked over, rinsed, and drained
1 tablespoon olive oil
1 large onion, chopped
3 cups low-sodium chicken broth
3 cups water
1 teaspoon salt
1 chipotle en adobo, mashed (1 tablespoon)

1. Soak the beans according to package directions.
2. Heat the oil in a large pot or Dutch oven over medium heat, then add the onion. Cook until the onion is lightly browned and tender, 4 minutes. Add the broth, water, and soaked beans. Bring to a boil, cover, and reduce heat to medium-low. Cook 40 minutes. Uncover, add the salt and cook, uncovered, until the beans are tender but still hold their shape, 20–40 minutes more. Stir in the chipotle.

Per serving (about ⅔ cup): 153 Cal, 2 g Fat, 1 g Sat Fat, 1 mg Chol, 242 mg Sod, 26 g Carb, 5 g Fib, 9 g Prot, 56 mg Calc. **POINTS: 2.**

FIVE-STAR TIP The cooking time for dried beans depends on their age and how they're soaked. So start checking the beans for doneness after 50 minutes, then check every 8 to 10 minutes, if necessary, until they are tender.

chicken sausage
canned black beans
canned diced tomatoes
instant polenta

QUICK LIST

Spicy Ragu with Polenta

MAKES 4 SERVINGS

Looking for an under-five-ingredient meal that's ready in under 15 minutes? This robust dish is chock-full of speedy ingredients—fully cooked chicken sausage, quick-cooking polenta, canned black beans, and spicy diced canned tomatoes with jalapeño peppers.

1 (8–9-ounce) package fully-cooked, lean chicken sausage (10% or less fat), cut into ½-inch-thick slices

2 (15-ounce) cans black beans, rinsed and drained

1 (14½-ounce) can diced tomatoes with jalapeños

3⅓ cups water

⅔ cup instant polenta

1. To prepare the ragu, spray a large nonstick skillet with nonstick spray and set over medium heat. Add the sausage and cook, turning occasionally, until nicely browned, 5–8 minutes. Add the beans, tomatoes, and ⅓ cup of the water. Partially cover and simmer until mixture thickens slightly and the flavors are blended, about 5 minutes.

2. Meanwhile, prepare the polenta: Bring the remaining 3 cups water to a boil in a medium saucepan. Whisking constantly, gradually add the polenta in a slow, steady stream; reduce the heat and cook until thick but not stiff, 5–6 minutes. Serve with the ragu.

Per serving (1 cup ragu with ⅔ cup polenta): 373 Cal, 11 g Fat, 3 g Sat Fat, 45 mg Chol, 1,221 mg Sod, 46 g Carb, 9 g Fib, 21 g Prot, 79 mg Calc. **POINTS: 8.**

FIVE-STAR TIP Fully cooked chicken sausage comes in a variety of flavors—sun-dried tomato and New Mexico-style are a couple of our favorites. Visit the butcher in the meat section of your supermarket and ask about the varieties he has available.

QUICK LIST

turkey cutlets
olive oil
onion
cherry peppers
chicken broth

Turkey Scaloppine with Peppers

MAKES 4 SERVINGS

Peppers of all kinds are an Italian cook's staple. This dish uses small, bright red cherry peppers (also known as Hungarian cherry peppers), which have a sweet flavor that can range from mild to medium-hot. Cherry peppers are most commonly pickled in vinegar, and their piquant taste adds zest to this easy sauté. Look for them in jars with the other pickled vegetables at the supermarket.

1¼ pounds turkey cutlets
½ teaspoon salt
3 teaspoons olive oil
1 large onion, cut into very thin wedges
¼ cup sliced cherry peppers in vinegar
¾ cup low-sodium chicken broth

1. Sprinkle the turkey with the salt.
2. Heat 1 teaspoon of the oil in a 12-inch nonstick skillet over medium-high heat, then add half of the turkey. Cook until lightly browned, 2 minutes on each side. Transfer the turkey to a plate. Repeat with 1 teaspoon of the oil and the remaining turkey.
3. Add the remaining 1 teaspoon oil and the onion to the same skillet. Reduce the heat; cook until the onions are deep golden and tender, 15 minutes. Add the cherry peppers and chicken broth; bring to a low boil. Cook until the mixture is slightly reduced, 5 minutes. Add the turkey and cook until just heated through, 1–2 minutes.

Per serving (¼ of turkey with about ⅓ cup peppers and onions): 221 Cal, 5 g Fat, 1 g Sat Fat, 103 mg Chol, 385 mg Sod, 3 g Carb, 1 g Fib, 38 g Prot, 24 mg Calc. **POINTS: 5.**

Turkey Scaloppine with Peppers

QUICK LIST

frozen shrimp
garlic
crushed red pepper
canned whole tomatoes
parsley

Shrimp Arrabbiata

MAKES 6 SERVINGS

This dish gets its inspiration from the Roman classic, pasta all'arrabbiata, which literally means "in the mad style." We're sure "mad" for this combo of shrimp and vibrant tomato sauce, which gets its kick from a liberal dose of crushed red pepper. Be sure the skillet is very hot before adding the shrimp, to lock in all its sweet seafood flavor.

1 (2-pound) bag frozen deveined shrimp, thawed and peeled

6 large garlic cloves, crushed through a press

1–1½ teaspoons crushed red pepper

½ teaspoon salt

1 (28-ounce) can whole tomatoes in juice, cut up and drained; reserve ¼ cup of the juice

¼ cup chopped flat-leaf parsley

1. Pat the shrimp dry with paper towels. Rub the shrimp with half of the garlic, the crushed red pepper, and salt combined in a bowl.

2. Spray a large nonstick skillet with nonstick spray (preferably olive-oil spray) and set over high heat. Add the shrimp and cook until deep golden, 1 minute on each side; transfer the shrimp to a large plate.

3. Add the remaining garlic to the same skillet; reduce the heat to medium and cook, pressing with a wooden spoon, until just fragrant, 20 seconds. Add the tomatoes and the reserved ¼ cup juice; bring to a boil. Reduce the heat and simmer until the tomatoes have thickened, about 12 minutes. Stir in the shrimp and parsley. Cook until the shrimp are just opaque in the center, 1–2 minutes.

Per serving (1 cup): 115 Cal, 1 g Fat, 0 g Sat Fat, 179 mg Chol, 542 mg Sod, 5 g Carb, 1 g Fib, 20 g Prot, 73 mg Calc. ***POINTS: 2.***

FIVE-STAR TIP   These shrimp make a lovely first course, or you can make the dish more substantial by adding a romaine or arugula salad or a side of wilted Swiss chard or spinach.

plum tomatoes
lime juice
scallions
ground ancho chile
sirloin steak

QUICK LIST

Chile-Rubbed Steak with Salsa Cruda

MAKES 4 SERVINGS

Discover the spice that chile experts have known about for years—ancho chile. Ground anchos are the dried, ground pods of capsicum peppers, which are indigenous to Mexico. Their mild heat and sweet, fruity flavor make this a perfect rub for steak, pork, or chicken. Ground ancho chile is available in Hispanic groceries and many supermarkets.

1½ pounds plum tomatoes (8 medium), diced
Juice of 1 lime
½ cup sliced scallions
1 teaspoon salt
1 tablespoon ground ancho chile
1 pound (1-inch-thick) boneless sirloin steak, trimmed of all visible fat

1. To prepare the salsa, combine the tomatoes, lime juice, scallions, and ½ teaspoon of the salt in a bowl; let stand while preparing the steak.

2. Combine the ground chile and the remaining ½ teaspoon salt in a cup; rub on all sides of the steak.

3. Spray a 12-inch nonstick skillet with nonstick spray and set over high heat until very hot, about 2 minutes. Add the steak and cook until meat is done to taste, 3–4 minutes on each side for medium-rare. Transfer the steak to a cutting board; let stand 10 minutes.

4. Slice the steak on an angle across the grain into twelve ½-inch-thick slices. Serve with the salsa.

Per serving (3 slices steak with ¾ cup salsa): 222 Cal, 8 g Fat, 3 g Sat Fat, 77 mg Chol, 675 mg Sod, 11 g Carb, 3 g Fib, 28 g Prot, 33 mg Calc. *POINTS: 5.*

FIVE-STAR TIP You can substitute regular chili powder for the ancho, but you may want to add ⅛ to ¼ teaspoon cayenne or hot paprika for more heat.

lo mein noodles
sirloin steak
chicken broth
hot pepper jelly
Asian hot chili sauce

Szechuan Steak with Noodles

MAKES 4 SERVINGS

Hot pepper jelly and Asian hot chile sauce gives these beefy noodles a double dose of heat. Look for hot pepper jelly that has bits of pepper in it (some varieties don't); you'll find it with the jams and preserves at the supermarket. Lo mein noodles can easily be found in Asian groceries.

½ pound lo mein noodles
¾ pound (½-inch-thick) boneless sirloin steak or beef top round steak, trimmed of all visible fat and cut into 1½-inch strips
½ teaspoon salt
¾ cup low-sodium chicken broth
3 tablespoons hot pepper jelly
1½ tablespoons Asian hot chili sauce

1. Cook the noodles according to package directions.
2. Meanwhile, sprinkle the steak with the salt. Spray a 12-inch nonstick skillet with nonstick spray and set over high heat until very hot, about 2 minutes. Add half the steak and cook, stirring, until browned, 1–1½ minutes. Transfer to a plate. Repeat with the remaining steak.
3. Add the broth, jelly, and chili sauce to the same skillet. Bring the mixture to a boil and cook until slightly thickened 10–20 seconds. Add the steak; stir until just heated through. Pour the mixture over the noodles.

Per serving (1½ cups): 402 Cal, 7 g Fat, 2 g Sat Fat, 58 mg Chol, 597 mg Sod, 56 g Carb, 3 g Fib, 28 g Prot, 22 mg Calc. **POINTS: 8.**

FIVE-STAR TIP If it's more convenient, substitute spaghetti for the lo mein noodles. Sprinkle the dish with sliced scallions for garnish, if desired.

Italian Hot Sausage and Swiss Chard Stew

QUICK LIST

plum tomatoes
pearl barley
Italian turkey sausage
garlic
Swiss chard

MAKES 4 SERVINGS

It only takes two lean hot turkey sausages to get a hefty jolt of heat in this hearty iron- and fiber-rich stew. We also stretched the flavor of fresh tomatoes by roasting them—a technique that brings out their maximum sweetness.

1 pound medium plum tomatoes, cut in half lengthwise
1 cup pearl barley
3¾ cups water
½ teaspoon salt
2 hot Italian turkey sausage links (10% or less fat)
3 large cloves garlic, crushed through a press
2½ pounds Swiss chard, rinsed and trimmed

1. Preheat the oven to 450°F. Line a broiler pan with foil. Place the tomatoes, cut-side up, in the pan; lightly spray with nonstick spray. Roast until softened and skins are charred, 20–25 minutes.

2. Bring the barley, water, and salt to a boil in a medium saucepan. Cook until just tender, 30–35 minutes. Remove the pan from the heat; cover and let stand until the liquid has been absorbed, 10 minutes.

3. Meantime, spray a large nonstick Dutch oven with nonstick spray and set over medium heat. Add the sausage and cook, turning occasionally, until browned and almost cooked through, about 10 minutes. Transfer to a cutting board; slice when cool enough to handle.

4. Add the garlic to the same Dutch oven and cook until fragrant, about 30 seconds. Add the chard with the water clinging to the leaves. Cover, increase the heat, and cook until the chard wilts, 5 minutes. Drain the chard; reserve ⅓ cup of the cooking liquid.

5. Return the chard and the reserved liquid to the Dutch oven; add the tomatoes and the sausage and bring to a simmer. Cook until the chard is tender and the tomatoes break into large pieces, 5–7 minutes. Serve with the barley.

Per serving (1 cup stew with generous ¾ cup barley): 298 Cal, 4 g Fat, 1 g Sat Fat, 15 mg Chol, 953 mg Sod, 55 g Carb, 14 g Fib, 15 g Prot, 162 mg Calc. **POINTS: 5.**

Fennel Pork and Roasted-Garlic Smashed Potatoes

fennel seeds
pork tenderloin
garlic
Yukon Gold potatoes
chicken broth

QUICK LIST

Fennel Pork and Roasted-Garlic Smashed Potatoes

MAKES 4 SERVINGS

Garlic and potatoes are natural partners, especially when they're served with this fennel-and-peppercorn-scented roast pork. To pump up the flavor, the crushed garlic cloves roast with the pork, then are mashed with the potatoes along with the pan drippings.

1 teaspoon salt

1½ teaspoons fennel seeds, crushed

1 teaspoon coarsely ground pepper

1 (1-pound) boneless pork tenderloin, trimmed of all visible fat

4 large cloves garlic, crushed

1¼ pounds Yukon Gold potatoes, peeled and quartered

1¼ cups low-sodium chicken broth

¼ cup water

1. Preheat the oven to 425°F.

2. Combine ¾ teaspoon of the salt, the fennel seeds, and pepper in a cup. Lightly spray the pork with olive-oil nonstick spray; rub the spice mixture on all sides of pork.

3. Spray a large nonstick skillet with nonstick spray and set over high heat. Add the pork and cook until browned on all sides, 5 minutes. Transfer the pork to a shallow roasting pan or broiler pan.

4. Place the garlic under the pork. Roast until the pork reaches an internal temperature of 160°F, 20–25 minutes.

5. Meanwhile, bring the potatoes, chicken broth, and the remaining ¼ teaspoon salt to a boil in a 3-quart saucepan. Cover and cook until tender, 16–18 minutes (do not drain.)

6. Transfer the pork and garlic to a carving board. Set the roasting pan aside. Finely chop the garlic. Set the roasting pan over medium heat. Add the ¼ cup water to the pan; cook, scraping up the browned bits from the bottom of the pan, until blended. Add the pan drippings and garlic to the potatoes; roughly mash with a potato masher. Slice the pork and serve with the potatoes.

Per serving (¼ of pork with about 1 cup potatoes): 262 Cal, 5 g Fat, 2 g Sat Fat, 68 mg Chol, 669 mg Sod, 26 g Carb, 3 g Fib, 28 g Prot, 32 mg Calc. **POINTS: 5.**

FIVE-STAR TIP   For more rustic-style mashed potatoes, leave the skins on but make sure they're well scrubbed. Substitute red-skinned potatoes for the Yukon Golds, if desired.

QUICK LIST

pineapple
lime juice
red onion
Jamaican jerk seasoning
pork tenderloin

Jamaican Jerk Pork with Pineapple Salsa

MAKES 4 SERVINGS

If you like your spice, here's great news: Jamaican jerk seasoning has never been more widely available in supermarkets than right now. A combination of chiles, thyme, and various spices (such as cinnamon, ginger, allspice, and cloves), jerk seasoning packs a flavor wallop when rubbed on grilled meats—especially on lean pork tenderloin. But it's also terrific on skinless boneless chicken breasts (coming in at *3 POINTS* per 4-ounce serving); just adjust the grilling time to 5 to 6 minutes on each side.

1 (1½-pound) pineapple, peeled, cored and cut crosswise into 1-inch-thick slices

2 tablespoons fresh lime juice

2 tablespoons finely chopped red onion

¾ teaspoon salt

1 tablespoon Jamaican jerk seasoning

1 (1-pound) boneless pork tenderloin, trimmed of all visible fat

1. Spray the grill rack with nonstick spray; prepare the grill.

2. To prepare the salsa, grill the pineapple until lightly charred, 3–5 minutes on each side. Transfer the pineapple to a cutting board and coarsely chop. Combine the pineapple, lime juice, onion, and ¼ teaspoon of the salt in a medium bowl. Set aside.

3. Combine the jerk seasoning and the remaining ½ teaspoon salt in a cup; rub on all sides of the pork. Grill, turning occasionally, until the pork reaches an internal temperature of 160°F, about 25 minutes. Slice the pork and serve with the salsa.

Per serving (¼ of pork with ½ cup salsa): 187 Cal, 5 g Fat, 1 g Sat Fat, 67 mg Chol, 695 mg Sod, 12 g Carb, 1 g Fib, 24 g Prot, 13 mg Calc.
POINTS: 4.

FIVE-STAR TIP Looking for a great way to cut down on prep time? Then check out fresh-cut pineapple in the produce section of the supermarket. It's available as peeled and cored cylinders or as spears.

garlic
honey
olive oil
cayenne
French bread

QUICK LIST

Caramelized Garlic Spread on Toasts

MAKES 9 SERVINGS

Calling all garlic lovers! This spread's for you. It's rich tasting, savory, and indulgent—with virtually no fat. How do we do it? By slowly cooking the cloves until golden brown to release every bit of their sweet, robust flavor. You'll need a dozen large cloves for the recipe, about 1 large head of garlic. For a festive presentation, garnish each serving with a sprinkle of finely chopped fresh rosemary or parsley.

12 large garlic cloves, peeled
⅓ cup water
1 tablespoon honey
¼ teaspoon olive oil or butter
¼–½ teaspoon cayenne
Pinch salt
Pinch freshly ground pepper
9 thin slices toasted French bread or water crackers

1. Fill a small saucepan two-thirds full of water and bring to a boil. Add the garlic and boil 2 minutes. Drain.
2. In the same saucepan, combine the garlic with the ⅓ cup water, honey, and oil; bring to a simmer. Cook the mixture over medium-low heat until the garlic is tender, 12 minutes. Add the cayenne, salt, and pepper; cook until the garlic turns deep golden, 2–3 minutes more.
3. Pulse the garlic mixture in a mini food processor until chunky and spreadable. Serve with the toasts or crackers.

Per serving (1 toast with 1 teaspoon garlic spread): 101 Cal, 1 g Fat, 0 g Sat Fat, 0 mg Chol, 208 mg Sod, 20 g Carb, 1 g Fib, 3 g Prot, 31 mg Calc. **POINTS: 2.**

FIVE-STAR TIP To make your own toasts, place slices of French bread on a baking sheet and broil 4 to 5 inches from the heat, 30 to 50 seconds on each side. For an extra flavor flourish, drizzle a few drops of premium aged balsamic vinegar over each serving.

Italian sweet peppers
white bread
oregano or parsley
extra-virgin olive oil
garlic

Italian Peppers with Rustic Garlic Crumbs

MAKES 6 SERVINGS

Known as Italian sweet or frying peppers, these long, slender peppers have a slightly sweet flavor that can range from medium to medium-hot. You can even add 1 tablespoon of grated Parmesan cheese to the crumb topping for the same number of *POINTS!*

12 Italian sweet, or frying, peppers (about ¾ pound)
3 slices firm white bread
2 tablespoons finely chopped oregano or parsley
1 tablespoon extra-virgin olive oil
1 large clove garlic, crushed through a press

1. Preheat the oven to 425°F. Spray a large jelly-roll pan with nonstick spray.
2. Place the peppers in a single layer in the pan; lightly spray with nonstick spray. Roast, turning once, until tender and lightly charred, 18 minutes.
3. Meanwhile, heat a large nonstick skillet over medium heat. Tear the bread into coarse crumbs (no larger than pea size). Add the crumbs and toast, stirring frequently, until dry and deep golden, 2–3 minutes. Cool.
4. Combine the crumbs, oregano, oil, and garlic in a bowl. Toss, gently rubbing ingredients together, to blend flavors.
5. Transfer the peppers to a platter and sprinkle with the seasoned bread crumbs.

Per serving (2 peppers with about ⅓ cup crumbs): 83 Cal, 3 g Fat, 1 g Sat Fat, 1 mg Chol, 89 mg Sod, 12 g Carb, 2 g Fib, 3 g Prot, 31 mg Calc. *POINTS: 2.*

FIVE-STAR TIP   You can also toast the bread crumbs in a 300°F oven. Place on a jelly-roll pan and bake, stirring once, until golden, 8 to 10 minutes.

| broccoli |
| lemon |
| red or green Thai chile |
| fresh ginger |
| garlic |

QUICK LIST

Thai-Style Broccoli

MAKES 4 SERVINGS

The smaller the chile, the hotter the taste—and that is certainly the case with the tiny "bird" chile peppers from Thailand. Thai chiles are fiery hot and have a wonderful flavor. The seeds, which produce the dominant heat, are usually not removed in Thai cooking. But you can certainly do so without the risk of sacrificing the rich flavor. Also, mature red chiles are generally milder than green ones because they sweeten as they ripen. Thai chiles may be purchased in most Asian groceries or in the produce section of some supermarkets.

1½ pounds broccoli crowns, cut into florets
Grated zest and juice of 1 lemon
1 red or green Thai or serrano chile, minced (wear gloves to prevent irritation)
2 teaspoons grated peeled fresh ginger
1 large clove garlic, minced
¾ teaspoon salt

1. Put the broccoli in a steamer basket; set in a saucepan over 1 inch of boiling water. Cover tightly and steam until bright green and tender, 5–6 minutes.
2. Combine the lemon zest and juice, chile, ginger, garlic, and salt in a large bowl. Add the broccoli and toss.

Per serving (1½ cups): 59 Cal, 1 g Fat, 0 g Sat Fat, 0 mg Chol, 483 mg Sod, 11 g Carb, 5 g Fib, 5 g Prot, 85 mg Calc. **POINTS: 0.**

FIVE-STAR TIP Both the dressing and the broccoli can be refrigerated up to two days ahead. Place the dressing in an airtight container. Steam the broccoli, cool, then transfer to a large zip-close plastic bag. Toss the broccoli with the dressing just before serving.

QUICK LIST

Chinese long beans
Asian sesame oil
garlic
Asian hot chili sauce
light brown sugar

Chinese Long Beans with Hot Chili Sauce

MAKES 4 SERVINGS

This dish uses Asian hot chili sauce for the kick and a touch of brown sugar to help brown the beans. If you can't find Chinese long beans, use an equal amount of green beans. Hot chili sauce is fiery, so start with the lesser amount and then add more if you can take the heat.

1 pound Chinese long beans, trimmed and cut into 6-inch lengths

1 teaspoon Asian (dark) sesame oil

2 large cloves garlic

1–1½ teaspoons Asian hot chili sauce

1 teaspoon packed light brown sugar

1. Place the beans in a large steamer basket and set in a large saucepan over 1 inch of water. Cover tightly and steam until bright green and almost tender, 5–6 minutes.

2. Heat the oil in a large skillet over medium-high heat, then add garlic. Cook, crushing the garlic with a spoon, until fragrant, 30 seconds. Add the beans and chili sauce; sprinkle with the brown sugar and cook, stirring, until lightly browned and tender, 2–3 minutes.

Per serving (1 cup): 51 Cal, 1 g Fat, 0 g Sat Fat, 0 mg Chol, 57 mg Sod, 10 g Carb, 3 g Fib, 2 g Prot, 49 mg Calc. **POINTS: 1.**

FIVE-STAR TIP Aromatic jasmine or basmati rice works beautifully with these beans. Cook according to package directions for four servings. With a fork, toss the rice with one tablespoon finely chopped cilantro and ½ teaspoon grated peeled fresh ginger.

5 MUST-HAVE KITCHEN GADGETS

There are all kinds of available cooking aids. But these terrific tools are selected to make your cooking easier, faster, and less messy.

Microplane Grater/Zester This stainless-steel, razor-sharp cutter makes grating hard cheeses, onions, bell peppers, and other vegetables a snap.

Instant-Read Fork Thermometer Insert this battery-operated device into food, and it instantly provides the internal temperature, ensuring that the item is cooked safely. This is a great gadget to use when grilling and roasting meats and poultry.

Mandolin Slicer Here's a perfect item to have handy for chopping, slicing, and grating. Its durable plastic frame holds a sharp, stainless-steel blade with attachments that can make thick or thin slices, julienne strips, or shreds. It easily cuts the prep time for vegetables in half.

Flexible Cutting Board This thin dishwasher-safe plastic sheet provides just as much support as a solid cutting board but can bend to funnel chopped foods into a bowl or skillet.

Garlic Peeler Say good-bye to garlic smells on your hands or smashed cloves. Simply place unpeeled whole garlic cloves inside this device's flexible rubber tube and roll the tube with your hand. Voila! The peeled cloves instantly pop out—ready for our splendid recipes.

Chapter 8

just desserts

go ahead, treat yourself!

QUICK LIST

bananas
butter
golden rum
dark brown sugar
vanilla frozen yogurt

Bananas Foster

MAKES 2 SERVINGS

Bananas Foster, that scrumptious concoction of sautéed bananas with rum, brown sugar, banana liqueur, and vanilla ice cream, was created at New Orleans's renowned Brennan's Restaurant in the 1950s. To give this classic a healthy makeover, we cut way down on the butter and sugar, and substituted low-fat vanilla frozen yogurt for the ice cream. The result? A totally decadent treat with no guilt attached. Because caramelizing bananas in a small amount of butter intensifies their rich flavor and velvety smooth texture, there's no need to search for overripe bananas to get great taste.

2 medium-ripe bananas
2 teaspoons unsalted butter
1½ tablespoons golden rum
2 tablespoons packed dark
  brown sugar
1 cup low-fat vanilla
  frozen yogurt

1. To prepare the topping, cut the bananas crosswise in half, then cut each piece lengthwise in half.
2. Melt the butter in a large nonstick skillet over medium heat. Add the bananas, cut-side down, and cook until golden brown, about 1½ minutes on each side. Add the rum and brown sugar; cook until sugar dissolves and mixture is syrupy, 1 minute.
3. Spoon the yogurt into ice cream dishes; divide the topping evenly over each serving. Serve at once.

Per serving (½ cup frozen yogurt with scant ½ cup topping): 302 Cal, 6 g Fat, 3 g Sat Fat, 16 mg Chol, 66 mg Sod, 60 g Carb, 3 g Fib, 6 g Prot, 173 mg Calc. *POINTS: 6.*

FIVE-STAR TIP For an alcohol-free version, substitute 1½ tablespoons apple cider with ½ teaspoon rum or vanilla extract for the rum. You can also easily double this recipe to serve four; just sauté the bananas in two batches.

Summer Pudding

frozen mixed berries
sugar
cassis
thin-sliced white bread
light whipped cream

QUICK LIST

MAKES 6 SERVINGS

For this classic do-ahead dessert, gently simmered strawberries, blueberries, and raspberries are piled into a bread-lined mold. If fresh berries are available, by all means substitute them for the frozen.

1 (12-ounce) package frozen mixed berries

⅓ cup sugar

2 tablespoons cassis or black currant syrup

10 slices thin white bread, crusts removed

¾ cup canned refrigerated light whipped cream or light whipped topping

1. Bring the frozen berries, sugar, and cassis to a simmer in a medium saucepan; cook 2 minutes. Set aside and cool to room temperature.

2. Line a 4 × 8-inch nonreactive metal or glass loaf pan with plastic wrap, so that the plastic wrap hangs 5 inches over the sides of the pan.

3. Cut 4 of the bread slices crosswise in half. Line the bottom of the pan with 3 of the half slices. Place the remaining 5 half slices lengthwise along the sides of the pan; trim the slices to fit.

4. Spoon about half of the berries and sauce into the pan; place 2 whole bread slices on top. Spoon in the remaining berry mixture; fold any ends of bread over the fruit. Top with the remaining 2 whole bread slices; cover the pudding with the plastic wrap. Place another 4 × 8-inch loaf pan directly on top of the pudding; weight the top pan down with a large, heavy can. Refrigerate at least 8 hours or overnight.

5. To serve, remove the can, the top loaf pan, and the plastic wrap from the top of the pudding. Invert the pan onto a serving plate; remove the plastic wrap and cut the pudding into 6 slices. Serve with the whipped cream.

Per serving (1 slice pudding with 2 tablespoons whipped cream): 214 Cal, 3 g Fat, 1 g Sat Fat, 0 mg Chol, 204 mg Sod, 40 g Carb, 2 g Fib, 3 g Prot, 40 mg Calc. *POINTS: 4.*

**Maple-Glazed
Pears à la Mode**

light sour cream
low-fat vanilla yogurt
pears
sugar
maple syrup

QUICK LIST

Maple-Glazed Pears à la Mode

MAKES 4 SERVINGS

To bypass the butter needed to cook the pears, we use a two-step process of first broiling, then roasting, the fruit to release its maximum flavor. We also skip the ice cream and prepare our own vanilla cream—a fabulous combo of light sour cream and low-fat vanilla yogurt. Bosc or Bartlett pears work well in this recipe, but you can also substitute apples with equally delicious results.

⅓ cup light sour cream
⅓ cup low-fat vanilla yogurt
4 firm-ripe pears, peeled, cored, and cut lengthwise in half
2 tablespoons sugar
¼ cup pure maple syrup

1. To prepare the vanilla cream, spoon the sour cream and yogurt into a coffee filter or cheesecloth-lined strainer; set over a bowl and let stand 30 minutes. Discard the liquid.
2. Meanwhile, preheat the broiler. Arrange the pears, cut-side down, in a 9-inch-square baking pan. Sprinkle the sugar evenly over the top. Broil the pears 6 inches from the heat until the pears begin to brown, 12 minutes.
3. Remove the pears from the oven. Reduce the oven temperature to 375°F. Drizzle the maple syrup over the pears. Bake until the syrup is bubbly and the pears are tender, 20 minutes. Spoon the vanilla cream into a bowl and stir until smooth. Serve the pears warm, drizzled with any pan juices, with the vanilla cream.

Per serving (2 pear halves with 2 tablespoons vanilla cream): 220 Cal, 3 g Fat, 2 g Sat Fat, 8 mg Chol, 28 mg Sod, 49 g Carb, 4 g Fib, 3 g Prot, 95 mg Calc. *POINTS: 4.*

FIVE-STAR TIP If you want to prepare the vanilla cream in advance, you can let the sour cream and yogurt mixture drain in the refrigerator up to two hours. You can also serve the pears at room temperature. For an elegant presentation, spoon the vanilla cream into the cored section of each pear half.

QUICK LIST

phyllo sheets
unsalted butter
Granny Smith apples
dark brown sugar
Asian five-spice powder

Apple-Spice Phyllo Cups

MAKES 6 SERVINGS

The phyllo cups for these easy-to-assemble sweets can be prepared ahead and stored in an airtight container at room temperature up to three days. Just recrisp them in a 350°F oven for 3 to 5 minutes. Want a party touch? Top each filled cup with 1 tablespoon light whipped topping for the same amount of *POINTS* per serving.

5 (12 × 17-inch) sheets phyllo dough, thawed according to package directions

1 tablespoon unsalted butter

6 (about 2½ pounds) Granny Smith apples, peeled, cored, and cut into thin wedges

¼ cup packed dark brown sugar

½ teaspoon Asian five-spice powder

Pinch salt

1. Preheat the oven to 350°F. Spray a 6-cup muffin tin and a small baking sheet with nonstick spray. Set both aside.
2. Stack the phyllo with the long side facing you on a work surface. With a sharp knife, cut the layered sheets lengthwise into two stacks of 6 × 17-inch strips.
3. Place one strip of the phyllo on a large cutting board; lightly spray strip with nonstick spray, then top with a second strip and spray again. (Cover remaining phyllo with plastic wrap to retain moisture.) With a sharp knife, cut the layered strips crosswise into 4 equal pieces. Gently press 1 piece, sprayed-side down, into 1 muffin cup, allowing ends to stand up. Repeat with 2 more pieces, overlapping pieces in spoke-wheel fashion so entire surface of the muffin cup is covered. Gently press the pieces into bottom of the muffin cup to fit. Repeat to make 6 phyllo cups. Slice remaining phyllo crosswise into small strips.
4. Spread small strips on the baking sheet and bake until golden, 8–10 minutes, as well as the cups, 15 minutes. Cool the cups in the muffin pan and the strips on a rack.
5. Meanwhile, melt butter in a large nonstick skillet over medium-high heat. Add the apples, brown sugar, five-spice powder, and salt. Cook, stirring occasionally, until liquid evaporates and apples are tender but still hold their shape, 20–22 minutes. Remove from heat and cool slightly.
6. Just before serving, spoon about ⅓ cup warm apple mixture into each phyllo cup and sprinkle with phyllo strips.

Per serving (1 phyllo cup with ⅙ of the strips): 191 Cal, 3 g Fat, 2 g Sat Fat, 5 mg Chol, 104 mg Sod, 41 g Carb, 3 g Fib, 1 g Prot, 18 mg Calc. *POINTS: 3.*

sugar
cornstarch
lemons
eggs
cream of tartar

QUICK LIST

Lemon Meringue Cups

MAKES 4 SERVINGS

Now you can enjoy the taste of one of America's favorite pies without all the fat and calories. To prevent the topping from "weeping" (forming beads of moisture on the surface), make sure to keep the filling hot while preparing the meringue.

1 cup sugar

3 tablespoons cornstarch

Pinch salt

1 cup cold water

3 lemons (to yield ⅓ cup juice plus 1 teaspoon grated zest)

2 large eggs, separated

⅛ teaspoon cream of tartar

1. Preheat the oven to 325°F. Place 4 (6-ounce) custard cups on a baking sheet; set aside.

2. To prepare the filling, combine ¾ cup of the sugar, the cornstarch, and salt in a medium saucepan; gradually whisk in the water until smooth. Cook over medium heat, whisking constantly, until the mixture comes to a simmer. Remove from the heat; whisk in the lemon juice, lemon zest, and egg yolks. Return the mixture to a simmer, whisking constantly. Remove from the heat; cover the surface of the filling with plastic wrap and keep warm.

3. With an electric mixer on low speed, beat the egg whites until foamy. Add the cream of tartar and beat until soft peaks form. Increase speed to high, and sprinkle in the remaining ¼ cup sugar, 1 tablespoon at a time; continue beating until stiff, glossy peaks form, about 2 minutes.

4. Spoon the hot filling into custard cups. Immediately spread the meringue over the tops, spreading to the edge of the cups and mounding in the center. Using the back of a spoon, make decorative swirls in the meringue. Bake until meringue is golden brown, 12–15 minutes. Cool to room temperature and serve, or refrigerate and serve chilled.

Per serving (1 cup): 259 Cal, 3 g Fat, 1 g Sat Fat, 106 mg Chol, 68 mg Sod, 58 g Carb, 0 g Fib, 3 g Prot, 15 mg Calc. **POINTS: 5.**

FIVE-STAR TIP   If you're concerned about cholesterol in the filling, eliminate 1 of the egg yolks and reduce the water by 2 tablespoons. You can also add a drop of yellow food coloring, if desired. This dessert may be refrigerated, loosely covered, up to two days.

QUICK LIST

plums
sugar
flour
allspice
pie crust

Plum Crostata

MAKES 8 SERVINGS

Here's a pretty, free-form tart that's deceptively easy to master. There's no special pie plate or double crust to mess with, and we use refrigerated pie dough. Try substituting other fruits—such as apples, peaches, pears, and apricots—so you can make this dessert year-round. When lining the baking sheet with foil, make sure it's at least a 14-inch square. (Use extra-wide foil or two sheets of regular foil.) That way you'll be sure to catch all the drips from the juicy filling during baking.

4 large plums (about 1½ pounds), halved, pitted, and cut into thin wedges

⅓ cup + 1 tablespoon sugar

1½ tablespoons all-purpose flour

¼ teaspoon ground allspice

1 refrigerated pie crust (from a 15-ounce package), softened according to package directions

1. Preheat oven to 400°F. Line a large baking sheet with heavy-duty foil; lightly spray the foil with nonstick spray.
2. To prepare the filling, combine the plums, ⅓ cup of the sugar, the flour, and allspice in a large bowl.
3. Between 2 lightly floured sheets of plastic wrap, roll the pie crust into a 13-inch circle. Uncover the top sheet of wrap; fold the circle into quarters and unfold onto the baking sheet. Discard the remaining plastic wrap.
4. Spoon the filling onto the crust, leaving a 2-inch border. Bring up the border and fold over the filling. Brush the border lightly with water; sprinkle the crust and the filling with the remaining 1 tablespoon sugar. Bake until the filling is bubbly and the crust is golden brown, 45 minutes. Cool on the baking sheet on a rack.

Per serving (⅛ of crostata): 213 Cal, 8 g Fat, 3 g Sat Fat, 5 mg Chol, 99 mg Sod, 36 g Carb, 1 g Fib, 1 g Prot, 1 mg Calc. *POINTS: 5.*

⭐

FIVE-STAR TIP Since the sweetness of fresh fruit can vary, taste the fruit first, then adjust the amount of sugar by 1 to 2 tablespoons, if necessary.

Plum Crostata

QUICK LIST

canned pineapple chunks
angel food cake mix
shredded coconut
raspberry all-fruit spread
raspberry liqueur

Pineapple Angel Food Cake

MAKES 6 SERVINGS

Angel food cake mix is a great convenience item to have on hand if you're looking for an extravagant dessert but want to keep the number of ingredients and fat grams in check. This cake gets its tropical taste from canned pineapple and shredded coconut. A lovely raspberry sauce is served on the side.

1 (8-ounce) can pineapple chunks in juice
1 (6.2-ounce) package white angel food cake mix
3 tablespoons shredded coconut
¾ cup seedless raspberry all-fruit spread
2 teaspoons raspberry liqueur or fresh lemon juice

1. Preheat the oven to 350°F. Place a sieve over a cup measure or small bowl. Add the pineapple and drain; set the juice aside. Cut the pineapple into small chunks. Return the pineapple to the sieve and set over the cup measure. Gently press out any excess juice with the back of a spoon.

2. Prepare the cake mix according to package directions, omitting the water specified on the box. With an electric mixer on medium speed, beat the cake mix and 6 tablespoons of the pineapple juice 1 minute. (Reserve any remaining pineapple juice for another use.) With a large rubber spatula, gently fold in the reserved pineapple chunks and the coconut until just combined.

3. Scrape the batter into an ungreased $4\frac{1}{2} \times 8\frac{1}{2}$-inch loaf pan. Bake immediately, until the top is golden brown and springs back when gently touched, 25–30 minutes. Immediately place the pan on one side on a rack and cool completely, about 1 hour. To loosen, run a thin-bladed knife around the edges of the pan. Invert onto a plate or cake rack, then reinvert right-side up.

4. Combine the fruit spread and the liqueur in a small microwavable bowl; microwave on High 40 seconds; stir until smooth. Serve the cake with the sauce.

Per serving (⅙ of cake with 2 tablespoons sauce): 196 Cal, 1 g Fat, 1 g Sat Fat, 0 mg Chol, 230 mg Sod, 43 g Carb, 2 g Fib, 3 g Prot, 98 mg Calc. *POINTS: 4.*

brownie frozen yogurt
cookie crumbs
honey
hot fudge sauce
light whipped cream

QUICK LIST

Frosty Chocolate Brownie Cake

MAKES 10 SERVINGS

You won't break a sweat making this celebratory dessert! We chose chocolate brownie frozen yogurt because it's chock-full of brownie bits, but you can certainly select another flavor. Or, if you like, make this a layered cake, using two different varieties of yogurt. If you go for the optional hot fudge sauce, add another *POINT* per serving.

2 pints low-fat chocolate brownie frozen yogurt

¾ cup chocolate cream sandwich cookie crumbs

1½ tablespoons honey

3 tablespoons fat-free hot fudge sauce (optional)

⅔ cup canned refrigerated light whipped cream or light whipped topping

1. Soften frozen yogurt in the refrigerator, 20–25 minutes.

2. Meanwhile, line an 8-inch round cake pan with 2 sheets of plastic wrap so that the plastic wrap hangs over the sides of the pan.

3. To prepare the crust, combine the cookie crumbs and honey in a medium bowl until blended. Set aside 2 tablespoons of the crumb mixture for the topping. Sprinkle the remaining crumb mixture evenly over the bottom of the pan; press down lightly with fingertips. Freeze the crust until firm, at least 10 minutes.

4. Spread the softened frozen yogurt evenly onto the crust. Cover the top with plastic wrap and freeze until firm, 1½ hours or overnight.

5. Remove the plastic wrap from the top of the cake. Line a cutting board with another sheet of plastic wrap; invert the pan onto the cutting board. Remove the pan and the plastic wrap from the sides and bottom of the cake; smooth the sides with a small spatula or knife. Invert the cake again onto a serving plate, remove the remaining plastic wrap, and sprinkle the top with the reserved 2 tablespoons crumb mixture. (Return the cake to the freezer until firm, if necessary.)

6. To serve, place the hot fudge sauce, if using, in a small microwavable bowl. Microwave on Medium until warm, 30 seconds. Drizzle the sauce on top of the cake and serve with the whipped cream.

Per serving (¹⁄₁₀ of cake): 214 Cal, 4 g Fat, 2 g Sat Fat, 4 mg Chol, 170 mg Sod, 39 g Carb, 1 g Fib, 5 g Prot, 120 mg Calc. *POINTS: 4.*

Double Chocolate Soufflés

sugar
eggs
cocoa
egg whites
chocolate liqueur

QUICK LIST

Double Chocolate Soufflés

MAKES 4 SERVINGS

It's surprisingly simple to put these lovely soufflés together; you just need to be organized. Be sure to have the ingredients measured and the mixer close by before getting started.

6 tablespoons sugar

2 large eggs, separated

1 tablespoon cornstarch

3 tablespoons cocoa

¾ cup water

2 egg whites

3 tablespoons chocolate liqueur

1. Preheat the oven to 375°F. Spray 4 (6-ounce) soufflé molds or custard cups with nonstick spray; dust the bottoms and sides with 1 tablespoon of the sugar. Cut four 8 × 3-inch strips of foil. Tape one strip of foil to make a "collar" around each mold that extends 2 inches above the rim. Spray the inside of each collar with nonstick spray.

2. Beat the 2 egg yolks with a fork in a small bowl; set aside. Combine 4 tablespoons of the sugar, the cornstarch, and cocoa in a medium saucepan. Whisk in the water until smooth. Cook over medium heat, whisking constantly, until the mixture comes to a boil and thickens, 2 minutes. Remove saucepan from the heat; gradually stir about ¼ cup of the chocolate mixture into the beaten egg yolks. Whisk the chocolate-egg mixture back into remaining chocolate mixture until blended. Reduce heat to medium-low; cook until thickened and just beginning to boil, 1 minute. Remove from heat; let stand 10 minutes to cool slightly.

3. With electric mixer on high speed, beat the 4 egg whites until foamy. Sprinkle in the remaining 1 tablespoon sugar; continue beating until stiff, glossy peaks form, 2 minutes. Gently stir about one-quarter of the beaten egg whites into chocolate mixture to lighten. With a rubber spatula, gently fold in remaining whites until just combined.

4. Place the soufflé molds on a jelly-roll pan. Spoon the batter into the molds; bake until puffed and firm to the touch, 18 minutes. Carefully transfer the soufflés to 4 serving plates. Immediately remove the collar from each, then make a small opening in the center with a spoon and add 2 teaspoons of the liqueur. Serve at once.

Per serving (1 soufflé): 173 Cal, 3 g Fat, 1 g Sat Fat, 106 mg Chol, 61 mg Sod, 28 g Carb, 1 g Fib, 6 g Prot, 19 mg Calc. **POINTS: 4.**

QUICK LIST

hazelnuts
sugar
cocoa
egg whites
cream of tartar

Chocolate-Hazelnut Meringues

MAKES 3 DOZEN MERINGUES

Light and delicious but loaded with the kind of rich chocolate and toasted-nut flavor that can only be called indulgent, these cookies more than satisfy. To ensure the cookies are light and crisp, it's important to pipe the meringues and get them in the oven as quickly as possible. So have your pastry bag and tip ready before starting to beat the whites.

⅓ cup skinned hazelnuts

1 cup sugar

2 tablespoons
Dutch-process cocoa

3 egg whites, at room
temperature

¼ teaspoon cream of tartar

1. Adjust the racks to divide the oven into thirds; preheat oven to 350°F. Place the hazelnuts in an ovenproof skillet or jelly-roll pan and toast in the oven until fragrant, about 8 minutes. When cool enough to handle, finely chop.

2. Reduce the oven temperature to 225°F. Line 2 large baking sheets with foil.

3. Grind the sugar until fine in a blender or food processor. Sift the cocoa and 1 tablespoon of the sugar into a small bowl; set aside.

4. With an electric mixer on medium speed, beat the egg whites and cream of tartar until soft peaks form. Gradually sprinkle in the remaining sugar, 2 tablespoons at a time, until the sugar completely dissolves and the whites stand in stiff, glossy peaks, about 8 minutes. On low speed, beat in the cocoa mixture until just combined. With a rubber spatula, quickly fold in the nuts; immediately fill with the meringue a large pastry bag fitted with a ½-inch plain tip.

5. Pipe the meringue onto the baking sheets, making 36 (1-inch) mounds, leaving about ½ inch between the meringues. Bake the meringues until they feel crisp to the touch, about 1 hour 30 minutes. Turn the oven off and leave the meringues in the oven until they are crisp and dry to the touch, at least 1 hour more.

6. Cool the meringues on the baking sheets on racks 10 minutes. Carefully peel meringues from the foil; transfer to racks to cool completely. Place meringues in an airtight container and store in a cool, dry place up to 3 weeks.

Per serving (1 meringue): 31 Cal, 1 g Fat, 0 g Sat Fat, 0 mg Chol, 5 mg Sod, 6 g Carb, 0 g Fib, 1 g Prot, 2 mg Calc. **POINTS: 1.**

cashews
cocoa
espresso powder
light cream cheese
confectioners' sugar

QUICK LIST

Cashew-Fudge Truffles

MAKES 24 TRUFFLES

Nothing beats silky-smooth, rich chocolate truffles for quelling an intense chocolate craving. Thanks to our surprisingly easy recipe, you can enjoy this wondrous confection with a clear conscience.

⅓ cup unsalted cashews

½ cup + 2 tablespoons cocoa

¾ teaspoon instant espresso powder or fine instant coffee granules

1 teaspoon water

Generous pinch salt

4 ounces light cream cheese (Neufchâtel), at room temperature

1½ cups confectioners' sugar

1. Preheat the oven to 325°F. Place the cashews in an ovenproof skillet or jelly-roll pan and toast in the oven until fragrant, about 8 minutes. When cool enough to handle, finely chop and set aside.

2. Sift ½ cup of the cocoa into a bowl; place the remaining 2 tablespoons cocoa in a small bowl for coating the truffles. Set both aside.

3. Combine the espresso powder, water, and salt in a microwavable cup. Microwave on High until the espresso powder dissolves, about 20 seconds. Scrape the espresso mixture into a medium bowl; add the cream cheese. With an electric mixer on medium speed, beat the mixture until smooth, 1 minute. Beat in the sugar until well blended. On low speed, beat in the ½ cup sifted cocoa, scraping down the sides of the bowl, until combined. Stir in the nuts with a wooden spoon.

4. Lightly spray a sheet of plastic wrap with nonstick spray; scrape the mixture on top of it. Shape mixture into a thin 12-inch-long log. Wrap well in the plastic, and refrigerate until the log is chilled through and slightly firm, at least 1 hour or overnight.

5. Sift the remaining 2 tablespoons cocoa into a shallow bowl. Slice the log into 24 pieces and quickly roll each piece, 1 at a time, into a 1-inch ball. Roll the balls in the cocoa to evenly coat. Refrigerate until firm, about 1 hour.

Per serving (1 truffle): 42 Cal, 1 g Fat, 1 g Sat Fat, 4 mg Chol, 32 mg Sod, 8 g Carb, 1 g Fib, 1 g Prot, 7 mg Calc. **POINTS: 1.**

QUICK LIST

eggs
sugar
crystallized ginger
flour
dried mango

Ginger-Mango Biscotti

MAKES 46 BISCOTTI

Who would believe you could make a cookie with just five ingredients—and virtually no fat! Finely diced crystallized ginger and dried mango are the sweet flavor boosters here, eliminating the need for an excessive amount of sugar. These cookies are lovely with coffee or tea, but if you want to dress them up a bit, drizzle with 1 ounce melted white chocolate. It won't add a single ***POINT!***

2 large eggs
⅔ cup sugar
¼ cup (1 ounce) finely chopped crystallized ginger
1¾ cups self-rising flour
2 ounces dried mango, diced (⅓ cup)

1. Preheat the oven to 350°F. Spray a large nonstick baking sheet with nonstick spray.
2. With an electric mixer on high speed, beat the eggs and sugar until pale yellow and doubled in volume, about 3 minutes. On low speed, add in the ginger and beat 1 minute. Beat in the flour until just combined. Stir in the mango with a wooden spoon. Refrigerate until dough is firm enough to handle, about 30 minutes.
3. Divide dough in half. On a lightly floured sheet of wax paper using lightly floured hands, pat one piece of the dough into an 11-inch log. Lifting the wax paper, transfer the log to the baking sheet. Repeat with remaining dough, placing the logs 2 inches apart on the sheet. Bake until golden and firm to the touch, about 20 minutes. Carefully transfer the logs to a cutting board; cool slightly. With a serrated knife, slice the logs ½-inch thick on a slight angle.
4. Arrange slices, flat-side down, on the baking sheet. Bake until lightly toasted, about 12 minutes. Cool completely on a rack; store in an airtight container up to 3 weeks.

Per serving (1 biscotti): 37 Cal, 0 g Fat, 0 g Sat Fat, 9 mg Chol, 64 mg Sod, 8 g Carb, 0 g Fib, 1 g Prot, 18 mg Calc. ***POINTS: 1.***

FIVE-STAR TIP Substitute your favorite dried fruit—apricots, pineapple, pears, figs, or golden raisins—for the mango. Although biscotti are traditionally twice baked, you can skip the second baking in our recipe. Just prepare the recipe as directed through Step 3, then let the biscotti air-dry on a rack until they reach desired crispness, about 24 to 48 hours.

Sweet-Wine and Watermelon Sorbet

MAKES 6 SERVINGS

Light, refreshing, and not overly sweet, this delightful sorbet can be served for dessert, or as a palate-cleanser between courses during a more formal meal. For an extra-special touch, present a small glass of Riesling wine to accompany each serving. The sorbet can be frozen for up to two months.

½ cup sugar

⅓ cup water

½ cup sweet white wine,
   such as Riesling

2¼ pounds seedless
   watermelon, cut into
   cubes (3 cups)

2 teaspoons fresh
   lime juice

1. Freeze an empty 1-quart airtight container.
2. Combine the sugar and water in a small saucepan and bring to a boil. Boil until the sugar is dissolved, 1 minute. Remove from the heat; stir in the wine. Cool.
3. Puree the watermelon and lime juice in a food processor or blender. Add the sugar syrup; pulse until combined. Strain the mixture through a fine-mesh sieve into a bowl. Cover with plastic wrap and refrigerate until chilled, 2 hours or overnight.
4. Freeze the chilled watermelon puree in an ice cream machine according to manufacturer's directions. Spoon into the chilled container; freeze until firm, at least 1 hour.

Per serving (½ cup): 119 Cal, 0 g Fat, 0 g Sat Fat, 0 mg Chol, 4 mg Sod, 25 g Carb, 0 g Fib, 1 g Prot, 8 mg Calc. *POINTS: 2.*

FIVE-STAR TIP If you don't have an ice cream machine, pour the mixture in a 9 × 13-inch metal baking pan or a shallow plastic container and cover with plastic wrap or a lid. Freeze until the sorbet is partially frozen, 2 hours. Stir to break up the ice crystals; cover and freeze until almost solid, 1½ hours. For a smooth texture, transfer the mixture to a food processor and pulse until smooth. Spoon into the chilled container and freeze until firm.

QUICK LIST

gelatin
sugar
apricot jam
low-fat buttermilk
light sour cream

Panna Cotta with Apricot Glaze

MAKES 4 SERVINGS

Italian panna cotta are sweet silky custards that are prepared with gelatin instead of eggs or cornstarch. We replace the heavy cream with a healthier blend of buttermilk and light sour cream, and flavor the custard with refreshing apricot all-fruit spread.

1¼ teaspoons unflavored
   gelatin
¼ cup cold water
3 tablespoons sugar
6 tablespoons apricot
   all-fruit spread or jam,
   strained through a
   fine-mesh sieve
1¼ cups low-fat buttermilk
½ cup light sour cream

1. Sprinkle the gelatin over the water in a microwavable cup measure or small bowl. Let stand 5 minutes to soften. Microwave on High until the gelatin dissolves, 40 seconds. Stir in the sugar and 3 tablespoons of the fruit spread; microwave on High until the sugar and fruit spread dissolve, 30 seconds.

2. Scrape the mixture into a medium bowl; whisk in the buttermilk and sour cream until smooth. Ladle into 4 (6-ounce) custard cups; cover each cup with plastic wrap. Refrigerate until set, 5 hours or overnight.

3. To prepare the glaze, place the remaining 3 tablespoons fruit spread in a small microwavable bowl. Microwave on High until the fruit spread just melts, 30 seconds. (The fruit spread should be fluid and just warm to the touch. If too hot, stir to cool.) Working with one panna cotta at a time, spread about 2 teaspoons glaze over the top of each. Refrigerate until the glaze is set, about 20 minutes.

Per serving (½ cup): 182 Cal, 3 g Fat, 2 g Sat Fat, 13 mg Chol, 114 mg Sod, 34 g Carb, 0 g Fib, 5 g Prot, 136 mg Calc. **POINTS: 4.**

FIVE-STAR TIP For an elegant serving option, remove each fully set panna cotta from its custard cup by first running a thin knife around the inside edge of the cup, then inverting onto a serving plate and shaking gently, if necessary, to loosen. Add the glaze and refrigerate, as instructed above, and serve garnished with fruit slices, if desired. To strain the apricot all-fruit more easily through a fine sieve, microwave the spread 20 to 30 seconds before starting.

Panna Cotta with Apricot Glaze

QUICK LIST

almonds
air-popped popcorn
sugar
vanilla extract
almond extract

Caramel-Almond Popcorn Balls

MAKES 8 SERVINGS

Want to have some fun in the kitchen and take a trip down memory lane? Make a batch of sweet, crunchy popcorn balls. We're nuts about the nutritional benefits of the almonds—an excellent source of the antioxidant vitamin E, as well as calcium, fiber, and the B vitamin folate. You'll need to pop ⅓ cup of corn kernels for this recipe.

½ cup sliced almonds
8 cups air-popped popcorn, unpopped kernels discarded
¾ cup sugar
Pinch salt
¼ cup water
1 teaspoon vanilla extract
1 teaspoon almond extract

1. Preheat the oven to 350°F. Place the almonds in an ovenproof skillet or jelly-roll pan and toast in the oven until fragrant and beginning to turn golden, 8 minutes. Set aside and cool completely.

2. Reduce the oven temperature to 275°F. Place a candy thermometer and a small dish of water with a clean pastry brush nearby. Spray a very large (6-quart) ovenproof bowl with nonstick spray. Combine the popcorn and toasted nuts in the bowl; place in the oven to warm as you start to cook the sugar.

3. To prepare the caramel, combine the sugar, salt, and water in a small saucepan and bring to a boil over medium-low heat. Boil, swirling the pan occasionally and brushing any crystallized sugar that forms on the side of the pan with the water, until the mixture just begins to turn golden and reaches 300°F (hard-crack stage) on a candy thermometer, about 4 minutes. Remove pan from heat; stir in the vanilla and almond extracts until blended.

4. Meanwhile, spray a large baking sheet and large metal spoon with nonstick spray. Gradually add the caramel to the warm popcorn mixture, tossing constantly with metal spoon, until evenly coated. Cool slightly, about 2 minutes.

5. Spray your hands with nonstick spray. When the popcorn mixture is cool enough to handle, quickly form into sixteen 2¼-inch balls; place on the baking sheet. Cool to room temperature.

Per serving (2 popcorn balls): 141 Cal, 3 g Fat, 0 g Sat Fat, 0 mg Chol, 18 mg Sod, 26 g Carb, 2 g Fib, 2 g Prot, 16 mg Calc. ***POINTS: 3.***

5 TIPS FOR KITCHEN SAFETY

1. Slow down. With the pressure of getting a meal ready in a hurry, now more than ever is the kitchen a perfect scene for an accident. So don't leave bags of groceries, stools, or anything else on the floor, where they can trip up a fast-moving cook.

2. Pay attention. Stay in the kitchen when cooking! Unattended cooking causes the majority of fires in the kitchen. So resist the urge to talk on the phone or go on the computer in another room while there's something happening on the stove.

3. Don't fuel the flame. If a grease fire starts, don't use water to extinguish it, as the fire will spread. Immediately cover the fire with a pan lid and turn off the burner. Without oxygen, the fire will die out.

4. Keep knives sharp. The number one reason for knife cuts is not improper use, but dull blades. A sharp knife will slide easily through what you're cutting, with little force involved, while a dull blade will just as easily slip off food, glancing off anything in its way (like your fingers).

5. Know the signals. Burns are often the result of things we can't see in the kitchen. So if you remove a hot pan or lid from the oven or the stovetop, leave a pot holder on the lid or utensil to warn others (and yourself) that it's hot. (And don't forget to let your friends and family know what the well-placed pot holder means!)

About Our Recipes

We make every effort to ensure that you will have success with our recipes. For best results and for nutritional accuracy, please keep the following guidelines in mind:

• All recipes feature approximate nutritional information; our recipes are analyzed for Calories (Cal), Total Fat (Fat), Saturated Fat (Sat Fat), Cholesterol (Chol), Sodium (Sod), Carbohydrates (Carb), Dietary Fiber (Fib), Protein (Prot), and Calcium (Calc).

• Nutritional information for recipes that include meat, fish, and poultry are based on cooked skinless boneless portions (unless otherwise stated), with the fat trimmed as specified in the recipe.

• All recipes include *POINTS* values based on the Weight Watchers **Winning Points** Food System. *POINTS* are calculated from a proprietary formula that takes into account calories, total fat, and dietary fiber.

• Before serving, divide foods—including any vegetables, sauce, or accompaniments—into portions of equal size according to the designated number of servings per recipe.

• Any substitutions made to the ingredients will alter the "Per serving" nutritional information and may affect the *POINTS* value.

• Additionally, substituting fat-free foods for any low-fat ingredients specified in a recipe may affect the consistency, texture, or flavor of the finished dish.

• If you prefer to avoid using alcohol in any recipe, you may substitute an equal amount of water, broth, or juice.

• It is implied that all greens in recipes should be washed or rinsed.

• All herbs called for are fresh, not dried, unless otherwise specified.

DRY AND LIQUID MEASUREMENT EQUIVALENTS

If you are converting the recipes in this book to metric measurements, use the following chart as a guide.

TEASPOONS	TABLESPOONS	CUPS	FLUID OUNCES
3 teaspoons	1 tablespoon		½ fluid ounce
6 teaspoons	2 tablespoons	⅛ cup	1 fluid ounce
8 teaspoons	2 tablespoons plus 2 teaspoons	⅙ cup	
12 teaspoons	4 tablespoons	¼ cup	2 fluid ounces
15 teaspoons	5 tablespoons	⅓ cup minus 1 teaspoon	
16 teaspoons	5 tablespoons plus 1 teaspoon	⅓ cup	
18 teaspoons	6 tablespoons	¼ cup plus 2 tablespoons	3 fluid ounces
24 teaspoons	8 tablespoons	½ cup	4 fluid ounces
30 teaspoons	10 tablespoons	½ cup plus 2 tablespoons	5 fluid ounces
32 teaspoons	10 tablespoons plus 2 teaspoons	⅔ cup	
36 teaspoons	12 tablespoons	¾ cup	6 fluid ounces
42 teaspoons	14 tablespoons	1 cup minus 2 tablespoons	7 fluid ounces
45 teaspoons	15 tablespoons	1 cup minus 1 tablespoon	
48 teaspoons	16 tablespoons	1 cup	8 fluid ounces

Note: Measurement of less than ⅛ teaspoon is a dash or a pinch. Metric volume measurements are approximate.

VOLUME	
¼ teaspoon	1 milliliter
½ teaspoon	2 milliliters
1 teaspoon	5 milliliters
1 tablespoon	15 milliliters
2 tablespoons	30 milliliters
3 tablespoons	45 milliliters
¼ cup	60 milliliters
⅓ cup	80 milliliters
½ cup	120 milliliters
⅔ cup	160 milliliters
¾ cup	175 milliliters
1 cup	240 milliliters
1 quart	950 milliliters

OVEN TEMPERATURE	
250°F	120°C
275°F	140°C
300°F	150°C
325°F	160°C
350°F	180°C
375°F	190°C
400°F	200°C
425°F	220°C
450°F	230°C
475°F	250°C
500°F	260°C
525°F	270°C

WEIGHT	
1 ounce	30 grams
¼ pound	120 grams
½ pound	240 grams
¾ pound	360 grams
1 pound	480 grams

LENGTH	
1 inch	25 millimeters
1 inch	2.5 centimeters

Index

Note: Page numbers in *italics* refer to photographs.

Notes

Notes

Notes